Cradles of Success

Cradles of Success
Britain's premier public schools

By
Mario di Monaco

The University of Buckingham Press

Cradles of Success first published in Great Britain in 2008 by UpFront Books

This second edition published in 2012 by

The University of Buckingham Press
Yeomanry House
Hunter Street
Buckingham MK18 1EG

A CIP catalogue record for this book is available at the British Library

ISBN 978190684066

Dedication

To my wife, Henrietta, without whose patience and support this book could not have been completed; and to my two sons, Henry and Jamie without whose schooling considerations this book would not have been started.

ACKNOWLEDGEMENTS

With any undertaking such as the writing of this book there are always a number of people who truly make it all happen. From the featured schools we are most grateful to, Barnaby Lenon, former Headmaster at Harrow, Anthony Little, Headmaster of Eton, Matthew Oakman, Director of Studies at Wellington and Anthony Seldon for allowing us to reproduce "Relax and Go with the Flow", Anthony Wallersteiner, Headmaster at Stowe. There were also a huge number of secretaries, registrars and admissions officers from every school who patiently answered our questions and gave up their time to meet with us. Emma Dandy, Financial Journalist gave us an important insight in how to fund education. Friends and their children who wrote about schools they had either attended or visited must be mentioned; Heather Morley, Barnaby Webster, John Bleekers, Keith Thomson, Robert Marshall, Andrew Crowston, Andrew Knott, Angus McCrorie-Shand, Isabelle Irwin and her mother Alex Irwin, Katie Crowston, Sandy and Robert Loder and James Estlin: my assistant, Kerry Rhodes, who painstakingly researched the schools. To all of you, many thanks.

Lastly and most importantly, my dear wife, Henrietta, thank you for your patience and encouragement, and of course my two boys, Henry and Jamie, without whom the motivation to write a book of this kind would have been totally absent!

The author and contributors have used school websites to support and confirm their original material and every effort has been made where websites have been quoted to reference appropriately; any failure to correctly reference is an oversight and we apologise.

CONTENTS

FOREWORD

Tony Little: Eton College

I AM very pleased to have been asked to write a foreword to Mario di Monaco's new book because in these pages he illustrates something of the rich opportunity and surprising diversity found in Britain's traditional public schools.

The lazy stereotype would have it that the best known of our public schools are the province of a narrow social group, that they are a closed shop and that tradition is a shackle, not a vibrant, living thing.

Tradition is important because it can inspire cultural depth and raise aspiration: in a school like Eton, which has educated young men for the best part of six centuries many of whom have gone on to achieve remarkable things, the implicit question is asked: 'Why not you?'. Informed by an unabashed belief in excellence and the virtue of being independent-minded, and shaped by the ideal of service, the best British public schools have aimed to launch young people into the world who believe in their ability to shape their own destinies and influence the lives of others for good.

In many ways these traditional schools have moved with the times, evolving their approach to teaching, changing technologies and adapting to the needs of a global economy, but they remain true to a distinctive ideal of education that values development of the whole person, not just the mind. In their philosophy, as with their governance and funding, these schools are free from government control; in this sense they are independent.

These leading independent schools choose to open their doors to young people of character and ability whatever their background. They continue to raise substantial sums of money to offer bursaries and scholarships to those who could not otherwise afford the fees in order to sustain a social texture that is to the benefit of each pupil. After all, young people learn at least as much from each other as from adults, and the composition of the student body is of central importance.

By whatever measure – academic performance, breadth of sporting and cultural activity, achievement in later life – the best British independent schools continue to show themselves as truly world class. Mario di Monaco gives his readers an insight into the nature of that success.

Tony Little

April 2012

INTRODUCTION

Mario di Monaco

I MUST make it clear from the very beginning that I am no great expert in this field and have no formal experience of having worked or taught in any school. My interest in writing a book of this nature stems purely from the fact that I have, for as long as I can remember, been fascinated by our famous public schools and in particular the way they have dominated the institutions of power and disproportionally influenced many areas of our national life. There are also personal reasons. We presently have two young boys at prep school and we are now in the process of selecting one or two suitable senior schools which we have covered in this book!

A fair few years ago I read medicine at University College London and I have been working as a full time doctor throughout my professional life. I am presently kept busy as the senior partner in a delightful medical practice located on the Hertfordshire /Middlesex border. Friends often ask why do I find public schools so interesting and where do I find the time to research the material required to write books on a subject unrelated to medicine. Of course time is always a scarce commodity, but if one is determined to achieve something which can simultaneously stimulate the mind and widen ones horizons, it is surprising how easy and enjoyable ventures of this nature can become.

My fascination with public schools goes well beyond the simple fact that they are there to educate children. Naturally, many of these institutions are architecturally striking and steeped in ancient history. This in itself can be a rewarding subject in its own right which I have found most enjoyable. However, there is a great deal more to learn about places like Eton, Harrow, Radley or Rugby than merely admiring their buildings or delving into their history. Much more interesting for example, especially for those of us who are not familiar with the closeted and rarified world of expensive boarding schools, is discovering how these "bastions of privilege" have shaped our class system and how this has affected the way we live in Britain. However, as engrossing as this subject may be, this book is not an appropriate vehicle for such a debate.

Choosing the right public school involves a great deal of homework and parents are advised to start early and avoid shortcuts. Making the wrong choice could profoundly affect your child's educational, personal and social development, as well as determine his or her future career prospects. With this in mind, we hope that a book of this kind, once read from beginning to end, will allow parents to gather some helpful preliminary information which can be used to compile a short-list of schools that they wish to explore further and those that they are happy to disregard. However, I must stress that this publication is not a definitive guide nor is it designed to provide all the information needed for a particular school. It is more of an introduction into a complex, bewildering and expensive journey. Furthermore, I must strongly emphasize that this book is most definitely not designed to substitute or undermine the prep school Headmaster/mistress extensive knowledge of senior schools. Parents should always turn for advice and guidance to the prep school Head. He or she will know a great deal more about your chosen schools than we could possibly cover in this book. Also, the Head, unlike any book you choose to read, will be aware of your child's academic ability, personality, sporting prowess etc. and therefore be able to recommend the most appropriate public schools on your chosen list.

So why the need for this book and what makes this book special? There is a wealth of information already available on public or independent schools as they now call themselves and the number of national glossy publications that periodically dabble in this subject is growing by the year. Furthermore, most schools now have excellent websites which can give a reasonably good outline of what the school has to offer. Having said that, our own experience in selecting a handful of prospective public schools for our boys' was certainly very instructive. Retrieving the massive amount of information available, both in print and online, was tedious and extremely labour intensive. A compact little book with all the important information condensed into readable articles would have been a great help. We therefore hope that by reading this book the task of selecting your preferred list of potential schools will be made a great deal easier.

Although time, resources and geography has made it impossible for me to visit all the schools we have covered, I have, much to my wife's amusement, managed to make it to the majority. Those that I have not visited have somewhat been trickier to write about but not impossible. Thanks to some painstaking research from Kerry Rhodes and yours truly, together with some helpful contributions from friends connected to these schools, past or present, we have been able to compile some fairly informative articles. Moreover, the book has been greatly enriched by individual accounts of parents' personal experiences of their old school such as Sandy Loder on Eton, Andrew Crowston on Oakham, Barnaby Webster on Bedford and Andrew Knott on Malvern as well as by pupils attending Rugby, Stowe, Tonbridge, Downe House and Eton. Heather Morleys' brilliantly written masterpieces on Wycombe Abbey and Tudor Hall make for compelling reading and so does John Bleeker's fatherly views on Canford, and the mother and daughter piece on Rugby school by the Irwin's family.

There are literally hundreds of good private schools dotted throughout the country and in an ideal world it would have been desirable to have included them all in this book. Obviously, such a monumental task would have been practically impossible to achieve given the constraints we faced. In the end, after careful consideration we decided to focus on a relatively small number of high profile, traditional public schools with a boarding ethos. In particular, those with a national and in some cases international reputation. Drawing up a shortlist was of course anything other than a precise science and the whole exercise proved to be difficult and contentious. Naturally, public schools such as Eton, Winchester, Harrow and Westminster would appear on anyone's shortlist, and so too would the likes of Radley, Rugby, Charterhouse, Marlborough, Wycombe Abbey and Cheltenham Ladies College. The cosmopolitan academic powerhouses of St Pauls Boys and St Pauls Girls have also been included since they are widely known and George Osborne our present Chancellor was educated at St Pauls. After all, we do not want to upset the man who has the power to set our tax rates!

The awkward question some may pose however, is why Tonbridge is in this book but not Sevenoaks or Kings Canterbury? Whilst acknowledging that the latter are excellent high achieving schools, if you were to ask the average man in the street which of the three Kentish schools mentioned above he was more familiar with, the most likely answer would be Tonbridge. Having said that there may be readers who will justifiably query why the likes of Berkhamsted School, Bedford and Merchant Taylors, all predominantly day schools have been included. The answer is simple and we make no apologies. The decision was based purely on economics and politics. These schools are local to us and we expect a large number of parents who reside within our area and whom we are acquainted with to purchase the book!!

So what has changed since my first book on this subject was published in September 2008? Cradles of Success, Britain's Traditional Public Schools rolled of the press almost on the day that the City of London went into financial meltdown following the collapse of a well know American investment bank. Such unfortunate timing might have dashed any hopes of a high ranking on the Amazon best sellers list, but from a parent's perspective, the prolonged period of job losses and stagnating growth that we have all endured over the last three and a half years has been far more of a concern. And yet, in 2012, many of our top boarding schools can charge £30,000 per annum and still boast long waiting lists. Clearly, even during a period of austerity when we are constantly asked by the government to tighten our belts, there seems to be plenty of people with enough money to send their offspring to the likes of Eton, Radley, Wellington, Marlborough, Stowe or Harrow. So in a nut shell, at least at the top end of the private educational pyramid, very little seems to have changed. Those commentators that were predicting the beginning of the end for private education have been proved wrong. Our top public schools remain the best in the world and continue to deliver a traditional and rounded education which parents from Britain and abroad, still value highly.

Finally, I would like to extend a note of gratitude to the real experts whose eloquently written contributions have added an exciting dimension to this book. A big thank you to: Anthony Little Headmaster of Eton College, Anthony Wallersteiner Headmaster of Stowe School, Anthony Seldon Headmaster of Wellington College, Matt Oakman Head of Studies Wellington College, Barnaby Lenon former Headmaster of Harrow School and Emma Dandy Financial Journalist. We hope that you will find this publication enjoyable as well as useful.

Good luck!

Dr M di Monaco April 2012

Part One

THE SINGLE SEX/CO-ED AND BOARDING/DAY DEBATE

Barnaby Lenon: formerly Headmaster of Harrow School

Single-sex/co-ed

OF THE 1,267 schools overseen by the Independent Schools Council, 133 are all-boy and 185 are all-girl; the remainder are all co-educational in varying proportions. The number of single-sex schools has declined steadily since 1970, mainly as a result of boys schools taking girls. Weaker boys' schools decided to take girls in order to fill empty places and improve exam results. Of course once they have decided to become co-educational these schools pretend that they made the decision on principle. But most know that the majority of the parents of their existing pupils would not have supported the change.

Every other year I do a survey of the attitudes of parents with sons at Harrow. The last survey I did showed that 96% were strongly in favour of Harrow remaining a boys-only school. Most pupils at Harrow have been to coeducational prep schools before coming to Harrow so their parents are not opposed to coeducation *per se*. But they are opposed to it, for both sons and daughters, during their *teenage years*.

There is plenty of evidence that co-education distorts subject choice. At co-educational schools girls are less likely to opt for science subjects and boys are much less likely to choose English or languages at A level.

1

Research by Professor Caroline Gipps showed that there are hardly any boys in Britain studying English A-level in mixed comprehensive schools – an extraordinary fact. Boys in co-ed schools do not choose English because it is seen as a 'girls' subject'. So the presence of the opposite sex is influencing subject choice. This is a pity: pupils should be choosing subjects on the basis of their ability and interests, not their self-image.

Both boys and girls appear to do better academically at single-sex schools. The coeducational schools have twice as many potential applicants as the single-sex schools, yet the league tables are dominated by single-sex schools. **Of A-levels taken by boys in 2005 at HMC independent schools, the proportion achieving a top grade was 37% at the co-ed schools but 52% at boys-only schools. The difference for girls was even more striking.**

In 2003 the government published the results of a research study conducted by the University of Cambridge which showed that boys achieved higher grades if taught in single-sex classes. Because of this, increasing numbers of mixed state schools are now segregating the sexes for teaching purposes.

Caroline Gipps' research showed that in single-sex schools there is likely to be less anxiety among boys about working hard and asking questions; in co-ed schools this was seen as something which should not be done in front of girls. Because girls mature earlier than boys and have better work habits, boys tend to be outclassed by girls in co-educational schools. Teenage boys have fragile self-esteem and they react by giving up the struggle to compete. All research shows that boys are less mature than girls from birth. This disadvantage makes boys less motivated especially when educated alongside girls, who are perceived as being cleverer and more diligent.

The Department for Education commissioned a team of educational specialists at Homerton College Cambridge to pilot a three year project. Working with schools around the country, it examined various ways of raising boys' achievement. In terms of single-sex teaching in English comprehensive schools they reported that:

- Pupils are almost always in favour of single-sex groupings, especially girls.

- Teacher opinion was divided, but most acknowledged greater levels of participation in lessons, and increased confidence amongst both sexes, in single-sex lessons.

- Teachers often felt that behaviour was better in single-sex groups.

Most teachers believe that boys and girls learn in different ways and should therefore be taught in different ways. Boys are keen to compete, girls learn better by co-operating. Boys tend to be over-optimistic about their academic potential, girls the reverse. Girls work harder, conform more readily and place a greater emphasis on neatness. Girls are much better at coursework. Boys benefit from tight structures and precise goals. Girls have superior verbal abilities, boys have higher numerical abilities. Boys prefer different sorts of books in literature courses.

Marion Cox, Head of English at the co-ed Cotswold School in Leicestershire, decided to do an experiment and teach boys and girls in single-sex classes. The result was that her staff was able to adjust their teaching styles specifically to suit boys or to suit girls, rather than striking a middle path between them. The number of boys scoring in the high range marks of the Key Stage 3 tests rose by a dramatic 400%. Boys found they could relax and express themselves more without girls present, and girls found the same. With a more suitable teaching style and a more focussed set of pupils, results improved.

These days teenage pupils have a pretty active social life in the holidays, half terms and during frequent *exeat* weekends. They do not need to have girls in the classroom in order to learn about the opposite sex. All boys and girls schools do activities with each other – dinners, dances, plays, joint musical events and joint plays.

Sport is much stronger in single-sex schools. Boys and girls do different sports at most schools.

If you halve the number of boys at a school you lose strength in depth and you can only field half as many teams. At Harrow we have had to drop several co-ed schools from our fixture lists because they cannot produce worthwhile competition.

In co-educational schools boys find it hard to compete with girls in cultural activities such as music. An average musical boy at a boys' school is much more likely to be in the orchestra than he would be at a co-educational school.

It is sometimes argued that it is 'unnatural' to segregate the sexes in education. In fact there is nothing natural or normal about putting hundreds of adolescent girls and boys together, particularly in a boarding school. My colleagues in co-educational schools have to deal with a spectrum of disciplinary and emotional problems arising from their coeducational status and this is a distraction from the main purpose of a school. Teenagers can do without the pressures of living alongside members of the opposite sex at a time in their lives of physical change and emotional vulnerability.

Because of the large number of boys' schools who take girls into their sixth form, almost all girls' schools lose some of their best students after GCSEs (for example, in London to Westminster, Latymer Upper and Highgate). This is tough on these girls' schools and all have reacted by improving the provision for sixth formers as a way of encouraging them to stay. Some girls clearly thrive in their new co-educational environment but others regret their choice, finding it harder to work effectively in a school which is dominated by boys and boyish attitudes.

Having said all of this, whether a school is single-sex or co-ed is clearly not the most important factor determining whether a school is a good one or not. The best co-educational schools (such as Rugby, Marlborough and Kings Canterbury) are excellent, the worst single-sex schools are no doubt bad. It is often convenient to have both sons and daughters at the same school. Many parents feel that there is much to be said for the best co-educational prep schools followed by a good single-sex public school.

Boarding or day?

Of the pupils in schools who are members of the Independent Schools Council, 442,000 are day pupils and 67,000 are boarders. Most of the boarders are over the age of 11, the biggest group being sixth-formers.

Boarding schools are expensive, £23 000-£26 000 a year in 2008, while independent day schools cost about half that amount (less at prep school level). In fact boarding schools make very little 'surplus' on their fees - often less than day schools – because they set their fees to just cover costs. But they are expensive.

There is little to choose between boarding and day schools in terms of academic results and in fact the structure of the academic programme in the two types of schools is similar. Boarding schools have two slight advantages: they do not have to have all their lessons between 9am and 4pm (they can have sport every afternoon when it is light and resume lessons between 4pm and 6pm), and boarding schools are more able to offer off-timetable lessons in the evenings (in Mandarin, Japanese, Russian, Astronomy and Art at Harrow).

Boarding schools have four big advantages:

* they are able to offer a much wider range of extra-curricular activities to a much higher proportion of pupils than day schools. Quite a few pupils at day schools do very little in terms of sport, music or drama but at boarding schools no pupils fail to engage in these types of activity at some level. This is the case not only because boarding schools have much more time at their disposal, but also because the House system provides more opportunities for low-level competitions. Also, boarding schools naturally attract staff who want to be involved in extra-curricular activity at a high level; many staff in day schools teach their subject and do little else.

* boarding schools often have a stronger sense of community, both at school and boarding house level. Friendships made at boarding schools tend to be deeper and longer-lasting.

* these days boarding schools look after pupils very well – the standard of pastoral care is often outstanding – and for teenagers particularly the quality of social life is often far healthier than that of pupils in day schools, especially those who live in cities.

* boarding schools can take pupils from all over the country and all over the world. This is an educational experience in itself – the opportunity to know people from many walks of life and from many different cultures.

And of course boarders do not have to travel to school, something which is becoming harder and harder in many parts of the country.

Boarding schools have some disadvantages. Pupils will not have the same level of privacy that they often have at home. The boarding environment is not for everyone and some older pupils find the loss of freedom quite irksome. The consequences of being in a boarding house with a group of pupils none of whom become friends are greater than the consequences of being in a day school class none of whom are your friends. Boarding schools are wonderful for the outgoing and active pupil, less ideal for the shy and non-sporty child. Some children are homesick and of course some parents dislike not being able to see their children every day. Some boarding schools have a large number of day pupils or weekly boarders and the full-time boarders can have a distinct feeling of being 'left behind' in the evenings and at weekends; such schools will also have less going on for pupils at weekends than the full boarding schools.

As with the co-education debate, however, there are good and bad boarding schools, good and bad day schools. Boarding schools exist in the twentieth century because of the excellence of their extra-curricular provision – but they are expensive.

NEWSPAPER LEAGUE TABLES OF SCHOOL EXAM RESULTS: THE PROS AND CONS

Barnaby Lenon: formerly Headmaster of Harrow School

SCHOOL exam league tables began in the national newspapers in the early 1990s. They sell papers and create a good fund of stories. They are a useful source of information for parents and a good measure of the average academic intake of a school.

The league tables have been a force for good in education because they have exposed under-performing schools. However, they have also had one serious negative effect: they have encouraged schools to put league table position at the top of their educational agendas. The schools which are normally in the top twenty of the league tables are under particular pressure to stay there – understandably so given the comments made in the media if one of them 'slips'. Nervous schools can do a number of things to improve their league table position:

* give little status to non-academic activities. Many of the most academic schools appear to offer plenty outside the classroom but in reality few of the pupils are involved or they are involved at a very superficial level.

* refuse to accept pupils who may have a great deal to offer but who are not highly academic. They accept a dull but intelligent pupil ahead of someone who is academically average but very good at music, say, or

sport. They will be reluctant to accept less able siblings or the children of former pupils.

* get rid of pupils who prove to be a disappointment academically.

* force pupils to drop subjects if they are struggling.

* encourage pupils to take 'easy' subjects and discourage them from choosing subjects which are known to be harder - such as modern languages, maths and sciences. (We know that some subjects are harder than others because the Curriculum Evaluation and Management Centre at the University of Durham correlates the average GCSE results of pupils with their A-level results. Pupils of a given GCSE score get a lower grade in subjects such as Chemistry than, say, Art or Media Studies). This is one reason for the popularity of the easy double-award science GCSE ahead of the harder single-subjects of Chemistry, Physics and Biology.

League tables say little about the ability of a school to improve its pupils prospects by teaching really well – what we know as 'value-added'. Value-added IS measured by the University of Durham every year (for individual pupils, for each academic department in a school, and for the whole school), but these figures are not made available for publication because Durham is rightly concerned that if their date is turned into league tables schools will manipulate the data to improve their position.

Some parents take league tables to be a measure of the teaching quality of a school. Of course in part they **are** a measure of this, but to a much greater degree they are a measure of the academic intake of a school. Some of the schools low in the league tables have been shown (by Ofsted and Independent School inspections) to have wonderful teaching and to be achieving excellent results given the low average academic ability of their pupils. This is true of some of the smaller boarding schools in remoter places who find it hard to attract pupils.

League tables tend to reinforce the position of schools – schools which come high in the league tables attract more applicants and so stay high. Schools which do badly in the league tables become less popular (possibly unfairly) and slip further down the list.

League tables do not take into account the fact girls achieve much better exam results. Girls' schools and mixed schools should do much better at GCSE and a bit better at A-level than boys' schools.

Parents sometimes fail to appreciate that a very small number of pupils can make a big difference to league table position. The newspapers often comment that 'school x' has slipped 20 places in the league tables as if this is a disgrace. In fact it may simply reflect the presence in that year group of a small number of less academic pupils – pupils who may be of great value to that school in ways which are not measured by league tables.

Newspapers publish their own league tables in August. The Government league tables of exam results are published in January. They are highly misleading. **Some of the schools with the best exam results appear low in the league table and many schools with rather bad results appear to have done rather well.** There are a number of reasons for this.

Sometimes pupils who take GCSEs under the age of 15 are not counted as having passed those GCSEs. In a school like Winchester, a highly selective school, this is a good proportion of the pupils – which is why Winchester comes relatively far down the league tables. In 2006 only 88% of their pupils were credited as having passed 5 GCSEs at grades A to C.

Although the government is now addressing the issue in the past the International GCSE has not been counted in the government league tables and so the most ambitious schools, which put pupils in for IGCSE because it is harder than GCSE and excludes coursework, are penalised. Many top schools, such as Harrow, Winchester and Rugby, who put pupils in for IGCSE maths, are recorded as having no passes in that subject!

The government is also addressing the issue where in the past vocational courses had the same or greater value than academic GCSEs. A Certificate in Cake Making had the same points value as Maths GCSE. GNVQ IT was scored as having four times the value of Physics or Greek GCSE. Colleagues of mine who have taught the GNVQ course say that it is a good course but it is ridiculous to claim that it is harder than a GCSE or that it has four times the content. The decision to weight these rather light-weight vocational courses in this way is a political one – to make schools with a weaker pupil intake look better than they really are.

So the August league tables are a good measure of the ability of the intake to a school but they do not tell you much about teaching quality and of course they tell you nothing about the many school activities which are not measured in public exams. The government league tables, which appear later in the year, are simply misleading.

HOW WILL I FUND THE SCHOOL FEES?

Emma Dandy, Financial Journalist

THIS is the big question for many parents. The cost of a private education is for many the single biggest financial commitment they will make and good planning, as far as possible in advance of the fees becoming due, is essential. For the lucky few, the cost of their children's independent education will never be a worry, either because their income is sufficient to cover the cost without reducing the family's quality of life, or because inherited wealth will be used to fund the fees.

For most parents the decision to educate children privately can cause a real financial headache. Suppose for a moment you have two children and plan to send them to a fee-paying boarding school from the age of 13 to 18. The five academic years of education for the two could well cost parents in the region of £265,000 at today's prices. That does not take into account all the extras that can be added to the bill including uniform, music lessons, school trips etc that can increase the cost of private education by roughly 10 per cent. The cost of this secondary education is likely to follow hard on the heels of nursery and junior schooling costs and ahead of the added burden of a university education. Overall, to educate one child in the independent sector at a day school from 5 years old up to the age of 18 could cost around £137,000.

To pay for a place at a senior boarding school – currently costing on average £8,500 per term – a 40 per cent taxpayer would need to ring-fence £42,500 of their annual salary before tax to cover the cost of the child's place, while a 50 per cent taxpayer would need to ring-fence £51,000. Multiply this by the number of children you have, or plan to have, and add in junior schooling and the sums involved can start to look frightening, particularly if you have other major financial commitments such as a mortgage to fund (not to mention everyday living expenses). Don't forget, either, that school fees have increased above the rate of inflation over the past few years – with annual increases of around 5 per cent on average – so if you are saving to pay for fees in the future they are likely to be well above today's rates.

TYPE OF SCHOOL	AVERAGE FEES PER TERM
Junior/Prep (5 to 11 years old)	
Day pupils at day schools	£3,289
Day pupils at boarding schools	£3,948
Boarders	£6,164
Senior (11 to 16 years old)	
Day pupils at day schools	£3,684
Day pupils at boarding schools	£5,030
Boarders	£8,347
Sixth Form (16 to 18 years old)	
Day pupils at day schools	£3,801

Day pupils at boarding schools	£5,430
Boarders	£8,782

Source: Independent Schools Council Census 2011

When planning how to fund your children's education it is also important to work out how the fees will be paid if family circumstances change dramatically. With the current economic climate remaining gloomy and unemployment on the increase, it would be sensible to have a contingency plan in place.

What will happen if the fee-payer loses their income due to long-term illness or redundancy, or in the event of the death of the person paying the fees? There are school fees insurance policies that can protect against such situations and life and health insurance for both the adults and the children can offer important financial protection.

For many families the only ways to fund school fees is to take on extra work – the second parent returning to employment, for example – or to use debt. In the past it has been possible to remortgage the family home to release equity to help pay the fees, but in a weak housing market and low growth economic environment this becomes a less attractive option.

A realistic budget of all household expenditure can reveal areas where cuts can be made, for example moving to cheaper car insurance. This will free up cash to help pay for fees currently due and reveal how much cash is left over each month that can be put away to help pay fees in future. Once parents have worked out how much they can put aside – either as a lump sum or on a monthly basis – it is important to consider whether investment plans offer good value. This can include looking at the safety of any capital invested, the level of risk involved, any tax breaks offered, hidden costs and the flexibility of the plan.

Depending on the options you choose to pursue, it is important to make sure that you take proper financial advice from an independent financial adviser, your solicitor or your accountant as rules on taxation etc are subject to change on a regular basis.

The Options

1. Savings Accounts

Clearly, as with any investment, the earlier one starts to put money to one side the better. The simplest option is to put cash into a bank or building society savings account. However, the returns that can be achieved on such savings – once tax has been deducted from interest earned and inflation has been taken into account – are not impressive. In fact there are currently no savings accounts that offer savers the chance to grow their money once the effects of inflation and taxation are taken into account. Instant access savings accounts currently pay on average just 0.9 per cent interest. Bank and building society savings rates are closely linked to the Bank of England's base rate, currently 0.5 per cent and unlikely to rise before 2014 at the earliest.

It is also important to remember that under the government-backed safety net of the Financial Services Compensation Scheme (FSCS) only the first £85,000 per person of savings in each UK-regulated financial institution are protected if the institution fails. And not all UK savings accounts are UK regulated and therefore are not covered by the FSCS scheme. For more details on which savings accounts are, or are not covered, check the Financial Services Authority's website at www.fsa.gov.uk

Using each adult's £5,340 annual cash ISA allowance is a good place to start saving. The Child Trust Fund and Junior ISAs are great for those saving for their children's future, but be aware that any cash invested in these two products can't be accessed until your child reaches the age of 18.

If one is looking for a better rate of return than savings accounts can offer, there are various options available. Holding a mix of different types of investment can also prove a good idea, as it will help to reduce risk.

There are many finance companies that specialise in investment schemes and tax planning for school fees, but make sure they are regulated by the Financial Services Authority. A simple search on the Internet will provide you with the details of many such companies.

2. Fees-in-Advance Investment Schemes

One type of investment product available allows parents to pay money into a school-run fund once a child's name has been placed on the waiting list. Paying into such a fund will not guarantee that the school will offer the child a place and the normal entrance requirements will still need to be fulfilled.

These schemes usually allow parents, grandparents or others to make lump sum payments in advance instead of paying fees as they come due. The payments can either cover a portion of future fees or the full amount. The rates of return achievable on these investment schemes may not be huge, one such scheme is currently offering a return of 2.7 per cent (equating to 4.5 per cent for a UK 40 per cent rate tax-payer), but most offer capital protection by limiting investment to government bonds or other fixed-interest bonds. However in these days of the Euro-zone governments' debt crises and increasing corporate debt default it may well be worth checking which bonds these schemes are investing your cash in. Rates of interest are often guaranteed, however, which is an advantage in the current low interest-rate environment.

Part of the attraction of the fees-in-advance policies is that schools can use their charitable status to make sure that tax is not paid on any interest. This is particularly attractive to higher-rate taxpayers who would normally pay 40 per cent tax, or the top 50 per cent tax rate on annual income over £150,000. Payments into these schemes should also be free from capital gains tax.

Inheritance tax liabilities must also be considered. Under current laws, payments into these schemes by a parent are exempt from inheritance tax while payments by other individuals are exempt provided the donor survives for seven years from the date of the payment. There are various other rules in place covering inheritance tax on gifts etc and it would be wise to seek professional advice.

When looking at these schemes, do read the small print. If the child does not gain a place at the school or their application is withdrawn, the money accumulated can usually be transferred to pay fees at another school. It can prove more difficult to get a refund paid to the donor, and in such situations the amount of interest paid on the cash invested may not be attractive. It is also important to check the small print to see if there are any circumstances under which a refund or transfer will not be made. Parents should take these issues into account when deciding whether such schemes are appropriate – particularly as entry to the school is not guaranteed.

3. Trusts

Paying for school fees from a discretionary trust can give real inheritance tax benefits for grandparents. These trusts can be used to transfer tax liability from the grandparent to the grandchild and make use of their annual income and capital gains tax allowances. Trusts are not such an attractive option for a parent paying school fees as any income from the trust is taxed as if it were the parent's income and not the child's.

The rules governing trusts – and the various different types that can be set up – are complex and it is important to seek proper professional advice if this route is taken.

4. Tax-Efficient Investments and Savings

If creating a trust is not a viable option, there are other investment options that offer tax breaks. The most popular is the Individual Savings Account (ISA), which many financial advisers consider to be the first place people should look to invest spare cash. ISAs allow anyone over the age of 18 to invest in a range of stock market investments or anyone over the age of 16 to invest in cash ISA savings accounts without incurring income tax or capital gains tax. The annual limits on investment in such products are subject to change but currently an individual can put away a maximum of £10,680 per annum per parent in an ISA provided that no more than £5,340 a year is held as cash. ISAs can form a useful part of an investment portfolio designed to fund school fees. It also means that this investment is available for other spending if necessary and is not ring-fenced for school fees.

As mentioned earlier, each child also has an annual income tax and capital gains tax allowance that can be used when investing, but do check the rules on how much a parent may gift to their child before tax is payable.

5. Shares, Bonds and Other Investments

The range of investment possibilities is seemingly endless once the tax-efficient options have been exhausted. Again, seeking advice from an independent financial adviser is essential. The potential returns on offer from such investments are directly related to the amount of risk one is willing to take on – but risk should be taken seriously. The FTSE 100 has increased in value by 4.1 per cent per annum on average over the last 10 years, but there have been many ups and sharp downturns along the way. Many fingers have also been burnt following the collapse of investments that were supposed to offer a sure-fire way to make huge profits. Parents have even been forced to withdraw their children from fee-paying schools or sell their homes after losing money when investments have gone to the wall.   Be wary too, as some attractive-looking investments may be fraudulent. Think of the $65billion fraudulent Ponzi scheme led by Bernard Madoff that engulfed many wealthy investors when it collapsed in December 2008.

The potential for decent returns is there if you know where to look, and the key is to spread the risk around and not put all your eggs in one investment basket.

6. Scholarships and Bursaries

For many children, bursaries and scholarships offer assistance with school fees. In 2011, one third of independent-school educated children received some form of financial assistance with their fees, with the average at £1,324 per pupil.

With the loss of the government-funded Assisted Places scheme some years ago, many schools have increased the number of bursaries available to help gifted children from lower-income backgrounds benefit from a private education. With a bursary the school will bear the cost of all or part of the fees provided the family agrees to be means-tested.

Scholarships are offered to children with a particular talent in music, sport etc or who are very academic. The award usually follows an exam or other assessment where the child will compete with others applying for the scholarship. Schemes vary but, like bursaries, can cover the full cost of the fees or just a portion. But beware, as scholarships are likely to be withdrawn if the child fails to remain a high achiever in the discipline for which the scholarship was awarded.

While scholarships and bursaries are available, it is unlikely that a family with more than one child will find themselves in the position where all their offspring's fees are covered. Advance planning is therefore still hugely important for all considering a private education and seeking sound expert financial advice is wise.

RELAX AND GO WITH THE FLOW[1]

Anthony Seldon: Wellington College

"I'M REALLY worried, sir," one of my pupils said to me a few years ago. "I've got four exams next week and I just don't know where to begin with my revision." With A-Levels and GCSEs on the cusp of commencing, thousands of young people will be going through a similar agony this weekend. To make matters worse, you probably will have been told by your teachers that it is harder than ever to get into the top universities; every grade in every subject matters. You can't afford to make any mistakes – and I really feel for you.

There are ways to negotiate the exam period though. It is crucial to adopt the right procedure. Ideally by this stage you will have boiled all your material down into compressed "revision notes" on postcards or mind-maps and you should be reading those repeatedly. You should also practise past exam papers, either on your own or with friends. Working with others is a vastly underutilised resource: if you're struggling to get your head around a topic there's nothing more lonely than revising on your own. Often when material is explained by somebody else rather than a text book, it becomes more deeply ingrained.

---

[1] Telegraph Weekend Saturday May 21st

In the exam hall the first 10 minutes are vital – bear this in mind as you walk in. Don't panic and start writing the moment you get the paper; instead read through all the questions carefully, underlining the key words. It's dangerously easy to make the mistake of answering the question in your head rather than the one staring up at you from the exam paper. Analyse the question fully, in all their elements. With essay questions, plan out a structured answer in bullet-point form which precisely corresponds to the question and then follow this plan. It also helps if you make a time plan: allocate an amount of time to each question depending on how many marks it is worth and keep a note of this on your desk. You should refer to it constantly as failing to finish a paper, like failing to answer the question set, is very common and yet totally avoidable. If a question – or the whole paper – seems unbearably difficult, do not panic. In all likelihood, it will be difficult for everyone else too. And if you think you have written a wrong answer, or a bad paper, don't chew over it. Time and again I have seen candidates mess up subsequent papers because they thought they had done badly on an earlier one. "Difficult" papers are often the ones on which you'll score the highest marks. Take a deep breath on the morning of an exam because none of the above techniques will work if you're feeling too stressed and tense.

We all know what it's like to play an important point in tennis or kick a penalty in football when you're wound up. Invariably you muck it up. So too with exams. You need to be in a state of "flow"; a condition of relaxed attentiveness where things happen naturally and easily. This is easier said than done. "How on earth can I relax when I've got these life-changing exams ahead of me?" my students ask me. I maintain that physical exercise is the best possible way to condition the mind prior to an important exam or an interview. Going on a run or doing some sort of sport two or three times a week throughout the exam period will help to clear your mind. Yoga and meditation are also great for preparing yourself for the day ahead; my pupils have got used to me standing on my head every morning.

There is no doubt that A-Levels and GCSEs are a fraught, high-pressure period but it's a myth that you have to shut yourself off from the real world to get through it. In fact, rather than working late into the evening, I advise pupils to watch television, chat to friends or even speak to their parents. It's also important to eat healthily, drink plenty of liquids and to go to bed at a decent time. At the end of the day, candidates should remember that whatever anyone tells you, these are only exams. Worse things can happen in life than not doing well. OK, so you may not get all A grades, and you might lose that place at Durham and end up going to Sussex or Sheffield. But the chances are you will survive. Remember the ultimate wisdom in life is to try your best, and then accept philosophically whatever happens after that. If your parents or teachers tell you otherwise, they are wrong.

Anthony Wallersteiner and Angus McCrorie-Shand: Stowe School

My First term at Stowe School

On my first day of year 9, I wondered how it was going to be possible to cope with the work, the size of the school, remembering all the teachers' names and being away from home for so long.

My previous school was very small in comparison to Stowe (almost as many boys in my house as were in my entire old prep school) so I didn't know what to expect but it soon became evident that I wasn't alone and that all year 9 pupils were in the same position as me. It was less daunting for me because joining me in year 9 and in my dorm was a best friend whom I went to nursery with and it was great that Stowe recognized this friendship and put us together.

However, quite quickly everything became much easier and more relaxed once I got into the swing of Stowe life, everyone welcomed me into the 'Stoic' community; I quickly made friends with the other boys in my dorm and house, Bruce. My House Master, Mr Sutton has been great and so far has known all the answers to my questions!

I signed up for several curricular clubs such as rugby, and I was also encouraged to join an extra curricular activity that I had never tried before which would stretch me, so I signed up for rowing, which I now really enjoy.

As I only live an hour away from Stowe my parents often drive up and watch my Sporting fixtures, music concerts and take me out for meals at the weekend and have even come in to tidy my dorm but I'm getting a bit more organized, more out of having to than wanting to!

I really enjoy Stowe and so quickly feel part of the school I hope that the next 5 years here will be as enjoyable as possible.

by Angus McCrorie Shand

I AM delighted that Angus McCrorie-Shand has enjoyed his first term at Stowe. Schools are dynamic communities in the literal sense that they evolve and change as each generation arrives with energy, promise, hope and possibilities. New pupils join schools full of bright optimism and creativity, happy to write a poem or paint a picture, not afraid to try out something new or acquire knowledge for knowledge's sake. Yet all too often they leave school as docile automatons, their intellectual appetites killed, minds saturated with bite-sized lumps of information downloaded from the internet and with little of sense of who they are, why they are here and where they are going. The challenge is to ensure that over the next five years Angus and his friends are not dragged down by the deadening utilitarianism which tells everyone that they need to do something "useful" and that the only way to achieve this is by passing exams at 11, 13, 16, 17 and 18. How many lessons can you remember which focused on exam revision when the teacher "taught to the test"?

Angus has already recognised that he has joined a pulsating community that is made of living flesh and blood which gains its character from pupils and staff, parents and governors. Instead of feeling lost, lonely and insignificant, Angus has been welcomed by "everyone" in the Stowe community. Pastoral care, administered and nurtured through the house system, ensures that the individual is always more important than the institution. Independent schools happily embrace a wide range of intellectual, sporting and cultural abilities with sportsmen and scholars, musicians and thespians, learning to respect each other, acknowledge their different talents and appreciate that everyone's contribution matters. Coming from a small prep school, Angus was nervous about joining a senior school with a roll of 780 pupils – yet entering a house of 65 boys (about the size of the roll of his prep school), made the transition much easier and he immediately realised that all the Year 9 pupils were facing the same challenges. Senior boys act as mentors to the younger boys who soon pick up the culture and credo of their house.

In Ethics, Aristotle defined friendship as a mutual affection, mutually known. Boarding offers more than just time together: children learn to live together unselfishly and form friendships that will often last a lifetime. Edges are rubbed off, independence discovered (I'm pleased to read that Angus is becoming more organised – even if this "more out of having to, than wanting to"). Being exposed to people from different cultures and backgrounds, with a variety of attitudes and beliefs, encourages tolerance and respect for diversity. Children living together with other children soon learn that people are not disposable objects, the ends do not justify the means and that they need to look beyond the self to find true happiness. They may be required to do things they don't always care for – compulsory chapel is a perennial discussion point at Stowe Council – but such activities often turn out to have lasting benefits. Stoics are provided with a framework of immutable principles and a liberal, humane philosophy rooted in Christianity and the Enlightenment. It is a moral and ethical compass that will serve them well in adult life as they take their place as citizens of the world.

A Religious Studies Common Entrance Paper once asked candidates to produce a survival guide for how to avoid being mocked in school. One answer went as follows: "always be late, never eat fruit or vegetables, always play games, always buy tuck, always watch the Simpsons, never do horse riding, never come first or last, always ride a scooter of skateboard, never wear elbow or kneepads". Angus' essay is striking in that he has happily signed up for activities that he had never tried before – rowing, for example – and he has not felt constrained by the need to conform. In addition to the key sports – rugby, hockey and cricket for boys and hockey, lacrosse, netball and tennis for girls – most independent schools offer a plethora of other activities: athletics, badminton, fencing, fives, sculling, golf, judo and, at Stowe, field sports which include clay pigeon shooting, equestrianism, fly-fishing and beagling. No one is humiliated for coming last or mocked for trying to acquire new skills and it is no longer essential to be good at games to enjoy popularity and esteem. Disraeli once observed that "were it not for music, we might in these days say the beautiful is dead". As a music exhibitioner, Angus is a member of chapel choir and a number of ensemble groups (including the "junior jazz combo") and he will be encouraged to expand his musical interests and repertoire as he moves through the school.

Angus pays tribute to the importance of his housemaster in helping him to settle in to his new environment and it is excellent that he has found someone who will be able to bring out his full potential. A prominent advertising campaign once proclaimed that no one forgets a good teacher: the best teachers have a genuine interest in their pupils, foster creativity and innovation, curiosity in science, technology and the arts, inculcate habits of deep thought, analysis, research and wider reading while passing on their expertise, enthusiasm and subject knowledge. We can correct our pupils until we get a grammatically perfect silence in the classroom, or the stillness of a practice room when a child has given up an instrument, but the only way of finding the limits of the possible is to encourage a child to be bold and to accept occasional mistakes and failure as necessary stages in the learning process.

A metaphysical force field radiates from an outstanding teacher, rippling through the boarding houses, academic departments, playing fields, theatres and recital halls as they unleash the potential, talent and intellectual energy of their pupils. Anyone who doubts the influence of a teacher should reflect on the words of Cardinal Williams: "an inspirational teacher flies with every pilot, builds with every architect, diagnoses with every doctor, creates with every artist, fashions with every craftsman and teaches with every teacher". Schools bring together the sum of knowledge from times past and present as an investment in time future. A school unable to produce independent learners willing to work things out for themselves, challenge the straitjacket of conventional orthodoxies, will be unable to teach them much else of value. As St Augustine wrote, "I learned best not from those who taught me, but from those who talked with me."

I recently visited the CERN laboratory in Geneva and was told by a prominent particle physicist that when a scientist tells you that something is possible, he is probably right; when he tells you that something is impossible he will almost certainly be proved wrong. By analysing the properties of the quark-gluon plasma in the first micro-seconds after Big Bang, searching for the elusive Higgs Boson particle, scientists at CERN are pushing the paradigms of particle physics and presenting us with hidden dimensions of time and space which may subvert our understanding of the laws of Nature. None of us can predict the twenty-first century counterpart to quantum theory, nuclear fission, the double helix and the computer – but we can be sure that there will be no major discoveries if schools stifle creativity, insist on rote learning and teaching to the test. We should all be depressed by a system of education which

31

takes little or no account of originality or individuality and which has stripped all sense of adventure and excitement from learning.

Angus will leave Stowe in 2016 and, in all likelihood, will be looking for a job in 2019 or 2020, probably retiring some time after 2060. He will be competing against graduates from China, Russia and India in an increasingly competitive and rapidly changing global market for employment. Our national wealth depends on the skills, knowledge and adaptability of our workforce. The UK will never be able to compete with labour costs or raw materials in countries like China and India and our manufacturing industries are unlikely to recover their former dominance. However, we can set the pace in intellectual capital and entrepreneurial flair, preparing our pupils, directly and indirectly, for work in international finance, legal and other services. We lead the field in creativity, music, the visual arts and technological innovation. Unless we support and nurture an education system that is the envy of the world, we will face a steady decline in prosperity and the future for pupils like Angus will be uncertain.

A Stowe education is about much more than the acquisition of skills to pass exams in order to get to the most prestigious universities and the best paid jobs. Stoics learn to generate their own ideas and think for themselves, rigorously and independently; they learn to appraise and appreciate beauty in art and music; they can hold a conversation, but they know when to listen; they are self-assured – but without the arrogance that often goes hand-in-hand with privilege. A root and branch reform of our schools is every bit as important as bringing down the national deficit. If the Coalition government is serious in its ambition to raise standards, roll back the state, give teachers greater freedom and allow more parental choice, the independent sector's unshakeable commitment to excellence and breadth of education provides a ready-made template for change.

Anthony Wallersteiner

THE QUALIFICATION DILEMMA

Matthew Oakman: Wellington College

IT USED to be so simple and easy; pupils studied O Levels and then on to A Levels before entering Higher Education. Now there are a myriad of differing and alternative qualifications that are available at both Key Stage 3 and 4. At the age of 14 students now have the choice of GCSEs or International GCSEs and in some cases the MYP (such as at Wellington College) which provides the middle school equivalent of the IB programme. Then, at 16, there are A Levels, the International Baccalaureate and the Cambridge Pre-U; all of which have their strengths and champions. It is a potentially confusing picture with parents and pupils quite rightly concerned about their individual merits and the regard with which HE hold them. This article will try to unlock this puzzle and provide a clear indication of the strengths of each of these qualifications and a rationale for choosing the course that suits the individual student.

GCSE, IGCSE or MYP

Many schools have now moved over entirely to the IGCSE and increasingly a number of independent schools are now offering the IGCSE in at least one subject. For many, the argument in favour of the IGCSE is that it is a more rigorous and demanding assessment in part because it is based on a final exam rather than the more modular GCSE equivalent where coursework is also built in to the final grade. Now that

33

GCSE has taken the modular route with coursework replaced by controlled assessments, some schools have decided that it lacks the necessary rigour and demand that will prepare the pupils for 6th Form and HE. The controlled assessments have also been deemed by some such as the Headmaster at Manchester GS, Dr Christopher Ray as "cumbersome and time consuming and they restrict the ability of schools to provide inspirational teaching for the most able pupils". It is clear that the reformed GCSE will benefit pupils of average and lower ability; it won't though provide the stretch that is necessary for the most able and talented students.

The IGCSE was criticised by QCA (Qualifications and Curriculum Authority) because it wasn't seen by them as being "suitable for assessing what pupils in England learn". There is some obvious truth in this given the fact that the IGCSEs are tailored for a multi-cultural, multi-lingual audience in a way that UK GCSE examinations are not. Some of the criticisms of the IGCSE range from the fact that there is insufficient prescribed reading for English, no speaking test for French and a lack of non-calculator examinations in Maths. QCA would argue that the GCSE syllabus was more in tune with the national curriculum programme of learning for all children aged 11-16 and thus a fairer and more appropriate form of examination.

Now that the government has reversed its ban on state schools teaching IGCSE, it will be fascinating to see if the trend towards IGCSE that has become apparent in the independent sector will be replicated. Sixteen state schools initially signed up in 2010 (with a further 50 schools expressing an interest) and this cohort will be taking their examinations this summer. It has coincided with the coalition government axing the diplomas that were instigated by the previous Labour government. This number has since grown substantially with 198 UK state schools now offering IGCSE with the result that 50% more schools entered candidates in the 2011 cycle. The coalition government have suggested that the changes to exams were primarily driven by ideological concerns and as Schools minister Nick Gibb said: "After years of political control over our exams system, schools must be given greater freedom to offer the qualifications employers and universities demand, and that properly prepare pupils for life, work and further study. For too long, children in state maintained schools have been unfairly denied the right to study for qualifications like the IGCSE, which has only served to widen the already vast divide between state and independent schools in this country. By removing the red tape, state school pupils will have the opportunity to leave school with the same set of qualifications as their peers from the top private schools - allowing them to better compete for university places and for the best jobs."

Whilst the IGCSE is undeniably growing in popularity with examination entries up 106% from 2010 to 2011, it is equally clear that the IGCSE doesn't fulfil the requirements of all schools or indeed all individual departments. For many, the GCSE is tried and trusted and has been the qualification of the majority of candidates since the first set of examinations in 1988. Here at Wellington some departments have chosen the IGCSE because it offers the stretch and demand that is most suitable in preparation for the 6th Form whilst others have continued with GCSE as they have deemed it appropriate and fit for the pupil body due to the apposite content material and the belief that it will maximise performance. The availability of choice is crucial so that the right course can be selected for the pupils to attain their very best.

With this last point in mind, Wellington College introduced the MYP (Middle Years Programme) in 2009 for all members of the 3rd Form (Year 9). At the end of this year, pupils could then opt to continue with the MYP or chose the GCSE/IGCSE route for the next two years. The MYP has enabled the College to create its own curriculum content that will stretch the pupil body in a manner that is free from the constraints of either GCSE or IGCSE. This has proved to be an exciting initiative that has allowed departments the freedom to create an invigorating and refreshing programme of academic study that allows the student body to explore the subject in a more independent fashion through a thematic approach. This can be best seen in History where students are studying revolutions and empires through the ages in MYP where they would be looking at events in isolation through either the GCSE or IGCSE. The programme consists of eight subject groups integrated through five areas of interaction that provide a framework for learning within and across the subjects. In the final year of the programme, students also engage in a personal project, an ideal preparation for the Extended Essay at IB or the EPQ as an addition to the A level curriculum. In this sense it provides both the freedom of curriculum and the academic stretch needed to ensure that the more able pupils are given the opportunity to extend themselves.

It is clear therefore that there are strengths within all of these different qualifications and schools will try to ensure that they are delivering the programme that is both suitable and apt for their pupil body. That is why we have decided that the preferred option for the Wellington pupils is to give them a choice to decide the path that they think is the most appropriate for them and the future of their academic studies.

Post 16 Options

The A Level has been under threat now for a period of time and in 2011 it no longer represented over 50% of the applicants through UCAS. The International Baccalaureate has grown considerably amongst the independent sector over the last decade and the Cambridge Pre-U has emerged as a further force in this increasingly competitive market. All of these have their proponents and it is undoubtedly a positive educational development that this variety of choices now exists in the post 16 sector. It is vital that students have a sensible range of choices because it is quite clear that there is a need for flexibility within the system and that these differing qualifications will suit a wide range of students.

The A level was seen as the gold standard in British schools for over 50 years but many are now questioning whether it lacks the necessary rigour and demand. Stephen Spurr, the head of Westminster School said that it had been forced to switch pupils to alternative qualifications "to stimulate" teenagers in eight subjects. He said that the Pre-U had "taken the lid off what we can achieve". This is borne out by the fact that five schools that were ranked in the top 20 after 2011 results offered the Pre-U or IB either alongside or instead of A Levels. In fact data from the Independent Schools Council showed that in 2011, 36 schools offered the Pre-U whilst 54 were delivering the IB.

At Wellington, the IB is offered alongside the IB reflecting the desire for choice with the knowledge that every child is an individual and there is no such thing as a perfect fit. We feel that A Levels still have great merit but have now taken the decision that all of those that take on this curriculum will also offer an EPQ (extended Project Qualification). This 5,000 word piece of research compares favourably with the Extended Essay, the 4,000 word equivalent which is part of the core element of IB and will enrich the A Level programme as well as making candidates more suitable for HE entry. It will allow all pupils in the 6th Form to undertake a piece of genuine research that will ideally be built around their desired area of study at university.

A recent study has been conducted comparing UK students who graduate from the IB diploma programme and those who complete A level courses. In the study, it was found that IB students on average are more likely to obtain higher paying salaries and achieve a higher level job than those who do A levels. Additionally, it was found that IB graduates are more likely to be admitted to one of the UK's top 20 Higher Education Institutions than graduates who took the A levels. A different study has concluded that top IB students perform better once they get to university than similar A level students. "In institutions with IB students having an average grade of 37 or more, for example, we find that the IB students are 5.4 percentage points more likely to achieve an upper second class degree or better," they say. There is no doubt that the IB is an excellent preparation for the demands of University and that for some students it is the ideal course for 6th form study.

A Levels though remain ideal for many students and it does allow them to specialise exclusively in their desired area of study and that has to be seen as a positive element of the course. The introduction of the A* has crucially introduced greater stretch and challenge to the course. The A* requires students to score 90% in their A2 modules, the hardest part of the course and thus represents a true test for even the most able students. They remain an excellent option for those who are dedicated to either the sciences, humanities or arts and don't want to continue with one or more of these components that are necessary within the IB.

It is though fair to conclude that A levels would benefit from further reform; Dr. Anthony Seldon writing in *Times Higher Education* earlier this year commented that the current system of GCSEs and A levels is "in deep trouble" due to the introduction of "bite-sized modules" that have "encouraged the culture of regular resits until top grades are attained. The content has been getting lighter, the examinations more susceptible to intrusive teacher and exam-board influence," he added. Dr Seldon accused schools, exam boards and successive governments of covering up the problems, with schools unwilling to "break their cosy oath of *omertà* about A levels." Addressing vice-chancellors, he said: "The three A grades that your departments are asking for your top courses are acquired more through rote learning than thinking." He added: "GCSEs and A levels are in deep trouble and we need you to stand up and say so if your universities are to recruit students who can think independently and love knowledge."

Pre U, A level and IB all have their merits. The key decision for any school or pupils is the selection of the course that best fits their desired route not only in the 6th form but also in preparation for HE. In the end it is the individual that matters and all schools should remember that when selecting 6th form courses that will enable every child to succeed to the best of their ability.

Higher Education

IB, A Level and Pre-U are all appropriate and effective pathways to Higher Education. Some have argued that universities favour either one or the other course but there is little evidence to back this up. As long as the pupil has chosen the course that is right for them and includes the subjects that are suitable and necessary for their university course, their application will depend on the quality of their personal statement, achieved and predicted grades as well as the nature of the reference given.

In four years of overseeing HE applications at Wellington, it has been encouraging to note that in the vast majority of cases, university selection is transparent and the right students will generally receive offers at the universities that are an appropriate academic fit. The one area that does cause difficulty is in the preferential treatment that seems to be given to overseas candidates (01 fee code) by certain universities where it is apparent that less able students are gaining places whereas more able UK students (02 fee code) aren't. This is in large due to the difference in the fee structure and the inevitable attraction of higher paying fee students who are on the 01 fee code.

It has also been interesting to observe the growth in applications to US universities over the last five years. This has been in part due to the reduction in the cost differential due to the implementation of tuition fees but also because of a growing sense that the more personal style of tuition with greater contact time in US universities offers better value for money. There can be no doubt as to the standard of education in US universities with their domination of the top universities in the world (QS ranks 51 US universities in the top 100). It has certainly been apparent at Wellington with 35 pupils sitting the SAT preparation course this academic year and up to 50% of the cohort in the lower school seriously looking at US universities at this stage. It is an exciting and invigorating alternative that pupils should continue to consider.

Conclusion

It is an exciting time within education and although the picture might look more confused due to the different qualifications available, in reality the pupils have greater choice and flexibility with their academic study than has previously been the case. The key to progression though comes with choosing the right curriculum to study for the individual so that it eases the pathway through to HE in a smooth and efficient manner where the pupils has the best possible chance to succeed. For some that will be IB, whilst for others it will be A Level or IB.

LIFE AFTER PUBLIC SCHOOL: KNOW YOUR UNIVERSITIES

Mario di Monaco

THE vast majority of pupils who are attending the schools that we have profiled in this book will eventually progress to one of the many excellent universities in Britain, or possibly cross the pond and head for one of the Ivy League Colleges in America. Naturally, having shelled out a large sum of money to educate their offspring at expensive boarding schools such as Winchester, Eton, Wycombe Abbey or Cheltenham Ladies, parents are likely to feel disappointed if their son or daughter ends up at some ex-polytechnic reading media studies. Not unreasonably, what many ambitious parents seem to want for their children is a place at a "top" university reading something traditional and challenging that is likely to lead to a glittering career.

So which are the fashionable and popular universities that seem to attract the best candidates from our top public schools?

Oxbridge

Founded over 750 years ago, Oxford and Cambridge are the oldest and most successful universities in Britain. For centuries, the "dreaming spires" of Oxford and the "backs" of Cambridge have attracted some of our most brilliant and ambitious scholars who have risen to the very top

41

of their chosen fields. So far, from the total of 55 British Prime Ministers to date, Oxford has educated 27 and Cambridge 14. In 2011 Cambridge was ranked first in the Q.S. World University Rankings ahead of Harvard in second place and Oxford came in 5th behind Yale in 4th place.

Clearly, our two most prestigious universities are world famous and not surprisingly they remain popular destinations for many talented public schools alumni. However, political pressure to widen access and increase the number of state educated students at Oxbridge has produced some interesting results. With fewer places available at Oxford or Cambridge for the independent sector, "middle tier" public schools have been squeezed and seen their numbers drop; whilst an elite group of academic schools like Westminster, Winchester, St Paul's and Eton have tightened their grip on Oxbridge and continue to send disproportionally large numbers to these top drawer universities. Anyhow, academic excellence does not stop at Oxbridge and failure to win a place at one of these ancient and prestigious universities should not been seen as having to settle for second best.

Golden triangle

The "Golden Triangle" is a term used to describe the university of Oxford and Cambridge which form two corners of the triangle and University College London and Imperial College London forming the third corner of this exclusive triangle. The London School of Economics and Kings College London are also seen as worthy members by some, but are not universally included by academic experts. Members of the Golden Triangle are highly ranked globally and enjoy an international reputation for academic excellence. In 2011 the Q.S. World University Rankings for the Golden Triangle members was as follows:

Cambridge - number one

Oxford - number five

Imperial College - number six

University College London - number seven

Kings College London - number twenty seven

London School of Economics - number sixty four

Golden Triangle Universities have very high research incomes and in many subjects such as Medicine, Law, Economics, Sciences and Engineering the top London Colleges are as good as Oxford or Cambridge and just as difficult to get in. Admittedly, an Oxbridge undergraduate experience is fairly unique and difficult to replicate anywhere else, but studying in London can be just as exciting and one's social life can be a great deal more hectic. Having spent five years at University College London reading medicine, I have a good idea of what the capital has to offer! However, whilst most would agree that London is a vibrant and cosmopolitan place, one needs to appreciate that it is also expensive, competitive and most definitely not a place for the insecure.

The Russell Group of universities

As from August 2012, the Russell Group will consist of 24 British research universities. Durham, Exeter, Queen Mary College London and York will be joining the other 20 universities. The original group which was considerably smaller than the present one, was formed in 1994, and first met at the Russell Hotel in Russell Square, London. Obtaining a place at a Russell Group university has become hugely competitive and most of the universities are oversubscribed. Nowadays, parents are well aware of the benefits of a Russell Group university education and will happily steer their sons or daughters away from independent schools that have a poor track record in sending students to these prestigious universities. This is understandable as one is now fully aware that there are employers out there that tend to recruit new graduates almost exclusively from the Russell Group. With this in mind, it is hardly surprising that the vast majority of public school pupils are keen to end up at one of these elite universities. The current membership of the group is:

University of Cambridge - World ranking 1

University of Oxford - world ranking 5

University College London - world ranking 7

Imperial College London - world ranking 6

London school of Economics - world ranking 64

Kings College London - world ranking 27

Edinburgh University - world ranking 20

Durham University

Manchester University - world ranking 29

Bristol University - world ranking 30

Leeds University - world ranking 93

Newcastle University - world ranking 127

Liverpool University - world ranking 123

Birmingham University - world ranking 67

Sheffield University - world ranking 72

Warwick University - world ranking 50

Belfast University - world ranking 193

Nottingham University - world ranking 74

Southampton University - world ranking 75

Glasgow University - world ranking 59

Cardiff University - world ranking 135

Exeter University

York University

Queen Mary College London

An Alternative

In a book about independent education it would seem appropriate to mention a comparative newcomer on the University scene, and one which adopts an increasingly interesting position in the market for university education. The University of Buckingham is the only independent university in the UK and is now 35 years old. And it is rising up the university league tables. Buckingham came 16th in the 2012 Guardian League tables and has come top in the National Student Survey for 6 years in a row. It prides itself on the provision of small group teaching on the Oxbridge model and its 4 terms a year 2 year degrees. It considers itself a teaching university and whilst it used to be considered expensive, especially after spending so much on independent secondary education, it now can be seen as being a more cost effective and faster route to a degree and the job market.

The "Rah" universities

Privately educated boys and girls, especially those who have attended high profile boarding schools such as Eton, Radley, Stowe, Harrow, Marlborough, Wycombe Abbey, Benenden, Rugby, Wellington or Oundle are amusingly referred to at university as "Rahs". A handful of British universities have gained a reputation for being particularly over-represented with "Rahs" and most Harrovians, Radleians, Etonians, Rugburiens etc. know exactly where to head for and which universities to avoid!

Naturally, anyone who is brave enough to compile a list of so called "Rah Unis" is likely to court controversy. However, I think that most people would agree that the following universities are all fairly "Rah":

Oxford

Cambridge

Bristol

Durham

Edinburgh

St Andrew's

U.C.L.

Imperial

Newcastle

Exeter

Leeds

A glance at Harrow school website will give one a good idea which universities Harrovians seem to favour. From 2000 to 2010 only 9 students went to Birmingham, 10 to Liverpool and 13 to Warwick. Astonishingly however, 167 went to Newcastle, 160 to Oxford, 149 to Edinburgh, 140 to Bristol, 116 to Durham, 99 to Leeds, 75 to Imperial College, 71 to Cambridge, 67 to U.C.L. and 42 to the L.S.E.

Clearly, some universities are very "Rah" and many are not. However, why Newcastle and to a lesser extent Leeds, have become magnets for public school students whilst the likes of Liverpool, Sheffield, Manchester or Birmingham have not, is a fascinating and intriguing question.

American Ivy League universities

An increasing number of students from out top public schools, especially the brighter ones who have missed out on Oxford, Cambridge, Imperial or U.C.L. are shunning the "lesser" British universities and heading for the famous and highly prestigious Ivy League universities all located in the Northeast region of the United States. Please note that other famous American universities geographically miles away from New England, such as Stanford in California and Dukes in Carolina, are NOT members of the Ivy League. Most of us are familiar with the globally renowned Harvard and Yale, but surprisingly there are eight universities that make up the Ivy League. The members are:

Harvard University

Yale University

Princeton University

Brown University

Columbia University

Cornell University

Dartmouth College

University of Pennsylvania

Ivy League Colleges are all private and charge much higher fees than the £9000 maximum which is the norm in England. However, they are all extremely rich and very generous bursaries are on offer to help with the fees. The likes of Harvard and Yale were once the preserve of the privileged and privately educated "Preppies" drawn predominantly from the WASP (White Anglo-Saxon Protestant) community. However, nowadays the Ivy League Colleges are more socially diverse and the main criterion for admission is academic excellence. The universities are all hugely popular and competition for places is fierce with an acceptance rate ranging from 5% to 20%. Like Oxbridge, the Ivy League Colleges have been dominant in politics and not surprisingly, the last four American Presidents have all attended Ivy League universities.

Part Two

The Schools

AMPLEFORTH COLLEGE

York Y06 4ER

www.college.ampleforth.org.uk

0143976000

ESTABLISHED in 1802 as a Catholic public school for boys, Ampleforth is commonly referred to as the "Eton of the North". The college striking buildings are perched on the edge of the North York Moors, with grounds extending to 2000 acres of outstanding natural beauty. The college is now fully co-educational and run by Benedictine monks and lay staff of Ampleforth Abbey. The 610 pupils are accommodated in 10 boarding Houses which have all been named after British saints. Girls now make up 30% of the intake and 85% of the pupils are full boarders. All the Houses are mixed age and single sex with the exception of St Aidan's the Sixth Form girls House. There are 7 boys and 3 girls Houses and facilities are of a high standard. Students eat their meals in their respective Houses and also play sports for their House. Great attention is paid to pastoral care and the school is keen to ensure that the boys and girls are well looked after and receive a truly rounded education.

Long regarded as the premier school for smart Catholic families from Britain and abroad, Ampleforth has educated a large number of high profile individuals ranging from the present Duke of Norfolk, to Rupert Everett the actor and Lawrence Dallaglio, who captained the victorious England rugby team during the 2002 World Cup. Interestingly, when Tony Blair became Prime Minister in 1997 and put Fettes College on the social map, some commentators began to refer to the latter as the so called Eton of the North. Whilst I have no wish to diminish the reputation of Blair's Alma Mater in anyway, I think that within the wider British community the Edinburgh public school does not quite live up to the media hype it enjoyed when New Labour were in power. Now of course, we have a Conservative Prime Minister who went to the real Eton, the "chief nurse of England's statesmen." Anyhow, for the purpose of this book we can perhaps conclude that Ampleforth should be seen as the Eton of the North of England and Fettes as the Eton of Scotland!

Moving on to academic matters, Ampleforth enjoys a good value added component and sends the vast majority of it students to good universities. Moreover, for a school that is not highly selective examination results are surprisingly good. People would be wrong to assume that because this school is miles from anywhere students are not pushed or expected to excel. As far as Ampleforth is concerned there is no such thing as a north/south academic divide and parents who chose this school can expect results comparable to its southern counterparts. In fact in 2011 the Financial Times Independent Schools Tables ranked Ampleforth 237th which compared well with Wellington College 220th, Uppingham 193rd, Rugby 172nd, and Haileybury 199th. The school most certainly outshone it local northern rivals Sedbergh 594th, and Stonyhurst 300th as well as southern schools such as Stowe 520th and Bradfield 401. Last year a respectable 7% of Amplefordians went on to Oxbridge. Naturally, like most other independent schools, Ampleforth takes the view that academic results should remain a top priority. However, the school is also keen to emphasise that the spiritual and moral development of their pupils is also high on their agenda.

There is officially no school uniform at Ampleforth, however there is a fairly strict dress code. Boys and girls wear black trousers or skirts with a navy, black or tweed jacket. Shirts must be smart and boys wear black or school tie. Many pupils move up from the college's own prep school, St Martin's Ampleforth. Entry is at 13+ and early registration is advisable as the list is closed when full capacity is reached. Once registered, the school will offer places up to 20 months prior to entry on conditions that the candidate achieves a 60% pass mark in the Common Entrance Examination or passing Ampleforth Entrance Examination. A report will also be requested from the prep school Headmaster. At 16+ (Sixth Form entry) places are offered on conditions that the prep school report is satisfactory and the candidate obtains a minimum of five GSCE's at grade B or better.

As one would expect from a Catholic foundation, a strong sense of faith permeates the school. Prayers are said daily in each House with a weekly mass in the Abbey Church. Right up to Sixth Form pupils are expected to study Christian theology and Christian living. Pupils are also encouraged to participate in local community projects and also ones as far afield as India or Africa. Furthermore, In addition to a Housemaster/mistress, each of the 10 Houses also has a priest assigned to it to ensure that the spiritual wellbeing of the students is not forgotten.

Ampleforth may be a long way from London, but, there is good evidence to suggest that an increasing number of southern families are looking to educate their children in northern schools of this nature. One of the main attractions seems to be the traditional full boarding nature of Ampleforth, which unlike many of the public schools in the south east, does not empty on Saturday afternoons after sport. This is a seven-day a-week boarding school which ensures that the week-ends are packed with activities and the all-in-it together attitude helps to foster solid and long lasting relationships. There are other reasons of course. Ampleforth is surrounded by vast expanses of beautiful country side and the distractions of big city life which affect many of the public schools in the south of England are absent. Also flash new money which is very much on display in schools close to London is not a major issue here. Ampleforth is more old money and pupils come from all over Britain. By the way, the annual boarding fees at Ampleforth stand at £27,400 which is slightly less than comparable boarding schools in the south.

Parental participation is encouraged and parents are allowed to visit at weekends and occasionally take their children home for the night. There are very few breaks other than half term and end of term holidays so to prevent any home sickness taking hold, it is important that children are not dropped off at the beginning of term and simply collected at half term. For those living in the crowded south east, a chance to escape to the unspoilt North Yorkshire countryside and breathe in some clean air should be enough to have you scuttling along the M1 or A1 as frequently as possible. With time you will get used to the bracing weather as you cheer your son on the rugby pitches!

The school has a great deal to offer away from the class room and an array of sporting, musical and culture activities are available. Some of the less common ones are gamekeeping and for older students the Wine Society! Rugby is played with real passion at this school and standards are high. Lawrence Dallaglio was, of course, brilliant enough to captain the England rugby team, but by his own admission, he apparently only ever played for the 2nd XV whilst at Ampleforth as he was not good enough for the 1st XV! The highlight of the sporting year is the annual rugby matches between Sedbergh and Ampleforth. Dallaglio has been quoted as saying that when he was at school Ampleforth did not lose any of the games against their rivals. However, in recent years Sedbergh have proved the stronger team.

In conclusion, a traditional boarding school with a liberal slant. Set in magnificent North Yorkshire countryside it has a great deal to offer the types who enjoy rural pursuits and games in the snow! Over the years it has educated many of the Great and Good and its list of famous alumni is impressively long. In the addition to the ones already named in this article, other well known Amplefordians include: Julian Fellows - actor and writer, Brigadier Andrew Parker Bowles, Joe Simpson - mountaineer and author, Cardinal Basil Hume, Edward Stourton - Journalist and Radio 4 presenter, Piers Paul Read - writer, John Crichton-Stuart - 7th Marquess of Bute "Johnny Dumfries" former racing driver, Andrew Festing - British Royal Potrait Painter and King Letsie III of Lesotho.

BEDFORD SCHOOL

De Parys Avenue

Bedford MK40 2TU

www.bedfordschool.org.uk

01234 362271

Barnaby Webster

BEDFORD School is an all boys school from ages 7-18. The school founded in 1552 is centrally located in the county town of Bedford, 50 miles north of London. Set in 50 acres of attractive grounds, it offers a wide range of impressive facilities, including its own observatory and planetarium, a £3million music school – one of the largest music departments in the country, a state of the art fitness centre and a refurbished cricket pavilion to name but a few.

There are around 1116 boys of whom the majority are day boys with around 274 boarding either full time or on a weekly basis. The school remains popular with overseas pupils with around 16 per cent coming from 26 different countries ranging from Europe to Asia. The majority of these are boarders. The school is one of several independent schools owned and managed by the Bedford Charity (the Harpur Trust). Boarding fees are £25,947 per year with day fees of £15,792.

Under the energetic and forward thinking leadership of Headmaster John Moule, Bedford School provides a well-rounded balanced education, and has endless opportunities for boys to explore. There is a strong focus on the pastoral care of the boys who all receive close support from a designated tutor under a house system. This allows the younger boys to grow and develop alongside the older ones. There are six boarding houses which each has an attached day house. Although there is a boarding ethos, Bedford is predominantly a day school, and therefore lacks the true boarding environment you would find at a more traditional boarding school.

Academic results have greatly improved over recent years under the leadership of the more recent Headmasters. Recent results show an almost 100% pass rate at GCSE with 60% at A or A*. Success rates at A level have also continued to improve each year with A & B grades at 82.24%. The school also offers the International Baccalaureate as an alternative to A levels. It performs well here with an average points score of 36.0, but this may be skewed by the fact that it tends to attract the brighter boys. Almost all boys go on to higher education with around 8% going to Oxbridge, approximately 10-15 boys per year.

Although these days the school now puts more emphasis on academic success, its real heart and soul still come from its sporting success. There is a huge range of sports to participate in at the school, but at the top of the table is the school's passion for rugby, hockey, cricket and rowing. Your success at these sports and especially in the case of rugby and cricket excel you into the higher echelons of the school's glitterati. With past pupils including ex-England rugby stars such as Martin Bayfield, Andy Gomarsall and cricket superstar Alistair Cook, the bar to succeed is set very high in these sports. Other noted recent ex-pupils also include the late Indy car champion Dan Wheldon, ex-Liberal Democrat leader Lord Ashdown and comedian Al Murray, showing how diverse old Bedfordians' careers can be.

Music and drama also play an important role in school life and with the school enjoying and on-site theatre as well as the new state of the art music hall. When not at school there are always plenty of tours for pupils to far flung places around the globe both for the sporty and the academic.

Bedford also maintains its close links with its military background, and professes one of the largest CFF corps in the country. Although "boys only", the school combines with the nearby Bedford Girls' School in many activities.

Although rightly or wrongly considered a division two public school, Bedford School certainly has made decent strides into propelling itself near the top of that division. It has many positive attributes and is one of those schools where you'd be hard pushed to find an activity that was not on offer – you can do everything from ballroom dancing to rifle shooting and there are not many schools that offer subjects ranging from Mandarin to Astronomy. As mentioned before, academic results have improved over recent years but it is still a far distance away from troubling the likes of Westminster or St Paul's. Hence why we find Bedford only ranking number 112 amongst the Financial Times 2011 Independent School rankings with 56% A*/A grades at A levels.

Bedford School is not the place to go if you want to mix with royalty and the landed gentry. Despite being sited in beautiful grounds, Bedford town itself is in general somewhat less attractive.

Bedford School is a solid all round school where opportunities are a plenty. It is not in the premier league of traditional public schools such as Eton or Harrow, although with its history of rowing and onsite fives courts it does brush hands with the public school elite. However, if you are looking for a school that will give you an all-round education but won't necessarily open doors to "high society" then Bedford School is certainly worth a serious look. It has a history of catering well for the overseas student and is fast becoming a popular choice due to the international opportunities it provides – offering the International Baccalaureate is an attractive alternative to A levels in the modern world. Although a less well known public school, it should certainly be higher up the "potential" list for would be parents. The best way to experience the school is to visit it in person and marvel at the wonderful facilities it has to offer.

BENENDEN SCHOOL

Cranbrook

Kent TN17 4AA

www.benenden.kent.sch.uk

BENENDEN School was established in 1923 by three former mistresses of Wycombe Abbey. As a full boarding school around 530 girls are accommodated in a total of ten houses, six for 11-16 year olds and four houses for the Sixth Form girls. Set in 250 acres of beautiful Kentish countryside you'd be forgiven for thinking that you were miles away from anywhere and yet the school is very conveniently located in Cranbrook just an hour and a half drive from London.

This amount of space has enabled the school to offer a vast array of sporting opportunities and the facilities are exceptional. Known as SPLASH (Sunley Pool Leisure and Sports Hall) this indoor facility houses a 25m pool, fitness gym – fully equipped, dance, aerobics and ballet studios as well as two sports halls and a suite of squash courts. Yoga, Fencing and Judo are just a few of the dozens of activities available. Outside there is an athletics track and field centre, lacrosse and hockey pitches and naturally netball and 11 tennis courts. Sport is very much part of the daily curriculum as well as being on offer as an extra curricula club. A high emphasis is placed on team sports and the school fields teams from A to D in most of the major girls' sports. In addition to the sports centre there has been a good deal of capital investment in recent years with a newly opened theatre and drama complex. Performances are taken outside of the school as often as practicable, either locally or even as adventurous as putting on "Me and My Girl" at the London Palladium. Two thirds of the girls learn a musical instrument and each week sees over

400 individual lessons. The next big opening will be the much anticipated Science Centre due to open in September 2012.

Benenden has always been a popular school and could boast a royal connection having educated Princess Anne. Its popularity though means that you need to be very organised should you be considering this as an option for your daughter. You really do need to register at least three years in advance for 13+ entry. Although it seems somewhat less pressurised if your daughter joins at age 11. Some people feel this is too young to be a full boarder but there are many girls who are mature enough to cope with being away from home and indeed the pastoral care at Beneden certainly smooths the path. Once your daughter has passed the Common Entrance, or if younger the schools own entrance exam, places are offered followed in the Autumn by a weekend stay at Benenden to get a feel for the boarding life. As soon as day one dawns each girl will be allocated a "Housemother", a girl in the year above them as well as a "big sister" who will be a Sixth Form girl to look after them in the first weeks and ensure a happy transition into their House. There is of course a resident Housemistress, matron and tutor to turn to should there be anything at all of concern.

In the 2011 Financial Times league tables, Benenden came in at 104 slightly better placed than rivals Roedean at 158th and Downe House at 123rd. However, it is interesting to note that all of the three schools mentioned had very similar Oxbridge "hit rates" at 14%, 13% and 15% respectively. Too much attention should not be paid to league table rankings for whilst they are a useful point of reference to assess a school it is the end game which will make a real difference to your child's future. If it is a top university place, either here or abroad, that you are hoping for then look at the academic subjects offered by the school and the scale of achievements in those. In 2011 of the 42 candidates from Benenden who sat Biology and Chemistry A-Levels 30 achieved A*/A grades. In Physics the A*/A result was awarded to 8 of the 9 girls. All 12 entrants for Further Mathematics had A*/A results and Mathematics saw 24 of the 35 girls achieving A*/A's. There are no "soft option" subjects at Benenden and the girls do very well.

There are strong social links with nearby Tonbridge School, although the girls have been known to desire Etonian boyfriends above all others! However, in summary this is a famous if rather "Sloaney" traditional full boarding school with an impeccable pedigree but certainly not to be seen as a finishing school for upper middle class girls. The high academic standards ensure that other than Oxford and Cambridge, Bristol, Edinburgh, Imperial and Durham also take a large number of Benenden leavers. This is a great school for all-rounders and if you live in London or the South East very well worth putting on to your shortlist.

Mario di Monaco with Kerry Rhodes

BERKHAMSTED COLLEGIATE SCHOOL

Castle Street

Berkhamsted HP4 2BB

www.berhamstedscollegiatechool.org.uk

SOME readers may ask why Berkhamsted School has been included in this book, largely devoted to more traditional boarding schools. But like Merchant Taylors Berkhamsted was once a boys' boarding school and has an ancient history dating back to 1541.

Berkhamsted School has undergone some rather big changes over the past three years. Under the Headship of the young and charismatic Mark Steed, who was previously headmaster at Kelly's in Devon, they have reverted back to their traditional name of Berkhamsted School. The board of Governors agreed to drop the "Collegiate" which had come about in 1998 when Berkhamsted Boys School founded in 1541 amalgamated with the somewhat younger Berkhamsted Girls School (1888) as well as the Preparatory School. With a new name came new branding, very smart uniform and the spectacular recently completed Nash Harris building at the Girls Senior School - Kings Campus - which houses a small chapel, a state of the art ICT suite, design and technology centre, a large dining hall and of course additional classrooms built around a beautiful grass quad. This was an investment in excess of £5 million, well spent as the school hopes to attract more girls to the senior school, which currently has around 400 pupils. It was announced in 2011 that Heatherton House, a girls prep school located in Chesham Bois near Amersham had been acquired by the Berkhamsted School Group, this arrangement may well see a number of families now seeing Berkhamsted Girls as the natural progression for their daughters.

Running on the diamond education model Berkhamsted has a co-educational prep school then at age 11 boys and girls are taught separately at the Castle and Kings Campus' respectively moving on thereafter a co-educational sixth form. The Castle Campus with just over 600 senior boys is interspersed with modern buildings but the overriding feel of the place is dictated by the original Tudor Hall built in 1544 and still in daily use, the cloistered quadrangle houses many of the common rooms and at one corner you will find the school Chapel, at which services are held weekly. Founded in 1541 it is an extremely old establishment based along the lines of a classic boarding school. All pupils are members of one of the 21 houses which operate as the first port of call in communications between parents and school and forms a valuable part of each pupil's school day. However of late it has become predominately a day school with a local catchment area. Parents tend to be professionals from the Home Counties, although there are an increasing number of families travelling in from North London. Berkhamsted is a very pleasant Hertfordshire market town and with around 1500 pupils in total the school is very much a thriving part of the town.

This school is in the enviable position of being the only private senior day school within a half hour driving radius of Berkhamsted. It is also just a few miles from the Buckinghamshire border and therefore familes considering this school may also have access to the Grammar school system. Until recently Berkhamsted School had the unfair reputation for being the repository for those children who had failed the 11+, this is definitely no longer the case. The school has become much more popular over the last eight or nine years and Mark Steed has increased the academic bar dramatically. Admission into the senior schools is taken by competitive entry, with priority being given to pupils who are already at the prep school. They write their entrance examinations in November prior to starting in September of the following year. Newcomers to the school are invited for interviews and to sit the entrance exam in January.

Entry into the Sixth form is again based on results with at least five B grades in the GCSE's being required – this holds true for existing students as well, so be prepared as over the past few years a number of pupils have had to leave at this stage if performance is not up to scratch. However that said teaching at this school is very highly rated and Berkhamsted is placed at a very respectable 200th place on the Financial Times league tables. There are two boarding houses, offering, flexi, weekly or full boarding. Both have been recently renovated to a high standard. Resident housemistress, matron, tutor and Chaplain ensure good pastoral care. Berkhamsted School markets itself very much as a community school.

With 40 acres of playing fields all the major sports are offered, rugby and lacrosse are particularly strong with boys and girls respectively being chosen to represent England on a regular basis. Tennis, squash, Eton fives, fencing, golf, shooting, cricket and hockey amongst others are also available. In 2004 a very impressive sports centre, the Knox-Johnston, was opened with a 25 meter swimming pool and fitness centre included.

Music, drama and art are well covered both in class and as extra-curricular activities. Academically Berkhamsted has very solid results, available showing boys and girls A level scores separately. It is pleasing to see that boys at least match and quite often outperform the girls. It's important to consider this when assessing co-ed schools that were formally boys' only institutions. Whilst not in the top leagues of Oxbridge entrants the majority of pupils do go on to good universities.

The current economic climate being what it is families with whom we are acquainted who had considered boarding have discovered that an equally good education can be obtained at day schools such as Berkhamsted for half the price, senior school fees are around £16,200. As more families evaluate their budget and also consider that academically Berkhamsted is on a par with Uppingham and Haileybury where day fees run at £19,800. However the comparison with other local day schools is not quite so favourable with results at Merchant Taylors ranking that school 35th on the Financial Times list, Haberdashers Aske at 20th for boys and 24th for girls. Berkhamsted has some way to go before really entering the big leagues. However this is a very popular local school, turning out bright and confident young people. If you aren't keen on full boarding and live within driving distance then Berkhamsted School should be on your list of schools to visit.

Mario di Monaco and Kerry Rhodes

BRADFIELD

Reading

Berkshire RG7 6AU

www.bradfieldcollege.org.uk

0118 964 4510

FOUNDED in 1850, this well established boarding school is set in the picturesque village of Bradfield, between Reading and Newbury in the heart of Berkshire. The charming brick-and-flint original buildings are located a stone's throw from Junction eleven of the M4,one hour from the capital and forty minutes from Heathrow. Such enviable geography has understandably caught the attention of the West and South West London "City Set" as well as the "Aga Set" from the Home Counties. Bradfield's reputation as a leading co-educational independent school stems principally from the extremely high standard of pastoral care on offer and it determination to look beyond academic achievements and focus on a broader and more holistic approach. That said, examination results are continually improving and the school now offers a choice of either the I.B. Diploma or A levels at Sixth Form Level.

For years, like many other British public schools established during the Victorian era, Bradfield was a boy's only boarding institution quietly getting on with the business of educating boys from relatively well off English homes. However, pressures to conform to new social trends as well as increased competition from rival public schools inevitably led to change, and in 2005 it became fully co-educational with girls now making up approximately 35 % of the intake. Many feel that the addition of girls has enhanced the reputation and popularity of this former bastion of male privilege. Others are bound to say that schools of this nature would have struggled to stay afloat if it had chosen to remain single sex. Of course, we will never know how things would have panned out and we can only speculate. All I can say is that this intriguing debate is beyond the scope of this book. Nowadays, well over 70 prep schools send pupils to Bradfield, and the school also happily welcomes boys and girls from abroad with some 15% of the intake now coming from overseas. Modern day Bradfield is not large and can best be described as a medium sized mixed ability establishment with numbers averaging around 740. The majority are boarders (85%) and the day pupils are fully integrated members of one of the boarding Houses. Clearly, Bradfield's boarding tradition remains robust and central to school life.

Although academic results are steadily improving, I think it would be fair to say that this school is most definitely not an "exam factory" or a gateway to our top ten universities. A glance at the Financial Times League Tables for Independent Schools reveals that Bradfield was ranked 401 in 2011. This compared well with Stowe at 529, St Edward's 483 and Pangbourne at 1273. However, Marlborough and Wellington, both co-educational schools "just off the M4" and with a similar historical and social pedigree to Bradfield, performed considerably better having been ranked 76 and 220 respectively. Also, as one would expect from a school that is not as academically selective as some of its competitors, in 2011 only four pupils made it to Oxbridge according to the F.T. Tables. However, parents need not despair. The teaching at Bradfield is reputed to be very good and the main objective is to deliver a first class rounded education which also values the importance of extra-curricular activities and the part they play in developing ones character. Furthermore, virtually everyone at Bradfield progress to some kind of "Uni" with a fair number winning places at prestigious Russell Group universities. It is also worth bearing in mind that in 2009 Bradfield received outstanding inspection reports from the Independent Schools Inspection team as well as Ofsted.

Admission to Bradfield is non discriminatory and fairly uncompetitive. Computer tests designed to gauge innate ability, such as the ones encountered at Eton or Wellington are not used at this school. The main points of entry are at 13+ into Faulkner's and into the vibrant and popular Sixth Form at 16+. Prospective parents are advised to visit the school on a Saturday morning during term time where they will tour the school and have an opportunity to hear a talk by the Headmaster and also meet a Housemaster or Housemistress. Parents who wish to pursue matters further need to complete a Provisional Entry Form and if known, state their preferred Senior House. At this point, it is worth mentioning that all the new entrance to the school at 13+ are housed in a state –of-the-art boarding House called Faulkner's which has been specially designed to help boys and girls make the potentially tricky transition from prep to senior school as smoothly and successfully as possible. After Faulkner's, the second year pupils move on to one of the 11 Senior Houses where they remain until they leave the school. This fairly unique arrangement at Bradfield is highly commendable and understandably valued by many parents.

Having completed a Provisional Entry Form this will secure a place on the school list. A follow up visit should then be arranged with your child when you will meet the Headmaster and spend time with the potential Housemaster/mistress. Twenty months before entry, and once the school has decided that your child is a suitable candidate, an offer letter of a guaranteed place will be sent out to you. This will be conditional on your son or daughter passing the Common Entrance Examination. For Sixth Form entry it is advisable to send your Provisional Entry Form early and admission requires a minimum of six GSCE's at grade B or above. Please note that a Bradfield education does not come cheaply. Current fees (2011-2012) are staggeringly high at £9,845 for boarders and £7,876 for day pupils.

Sport is important at Bradfield and they are proudly very competitive. Surprisingly for a public school there is no rugby. The major boys' sports are football, cricket and hockey, with girls enjoying hockey, lacrosse, netball and tennis. There is a lot of choice in secondary sports like polo, squash, fives, fencing, swimming and clay shooting. Football is the main winter activity for boys and Bradfield deservedly enjoys a great reputation in this sport. This perhaps explains the rumours that Brooklyn, the son of the ex-England football legend David Beckham, is down to join Bradfield. In general the sporting facilities are exceptional and there is a sports complex with indoor swimming pool and tennis centre as well as two floodlit all weather pitches. A golf course and superb playing fields overlooking the Pang valley all add to the attraction.

Despite all the sporting and extra-curricular activities, Bradfield is probably most well known for its Greek theatre and staging of Greek plays. These take place on a three-year rota shared with Oxford and Cambridge, in which students have nine months to learn the lines, all in ancient Greek, and perform to packed audiences. These plays were started 150 years ago by the Headmaster Dr Herbert Branston-Gray to save the school from bankruptcy! The 2009 Greek play, which was performed at Bradfield and the end of June and beginning of July, was Oedipus by Sophocles.

Contemporary Bradfield is an exciting and forward looking school which strives to combine values and attributes essential for the 21st century. The school enjoys a reputation for being friendly and unpretentious and pupils are drawn from varied social backgrounds resulting in a community with diverse talents but shared attitudes. The wonderful chapel is a constant reminder of the strong Anglican foundation and remains central to the spiritual, reflective and moral philosophies of this school as set out by Thomas Stevens, who established Bradfield in 1850. After-school clubs and activities cover all sorts of options from the highly commendable Community Service Volunteers, who help in the local community, to the Duke of Edinburgh Awards and CCF.

In September 2011 Bradfield College appointed a new Headmaster, Simon Henderson to succeed Peter Roberts. Simon, who was educated at Winchester College and Brasenose College, Oxford, was formerly Deputy Head at Sherborne School, prior to which he had held the position of Head of History at Eton College. We send our best wishes.

Finally, it is worth noting that this school has educated many famous people and a quick glance at the list of Notable Old Bradfieldians will reveal names such as: Louis de Bernieres ,the novelist who wrote Captain Correlli's Mandolin, Lord David Owen, Politician and founder member of the Social Democratic Party in the 1980's, Nick Clarke, journalist and BBC Radio 4 presenter who died in 2006, Tony Hancock, famous comedian who died in 1968, Sir John Nott who served in Mrs Thatcher's Cabinet in the 1980's, Claudia Harrison, actress and Ronald Muwenda Mutebi II, current King of Buganda.

WITH its grade 1 listed manor house set in 250 acres and architectural roots that date back to Saxon times, the Norman church in the grounds and John O'Gaunt's kitchen that dates back to the 14th century still survive. The main building, now the heart of the school, designed by Edward Blore and later Sir Charles Barry, dates back to the 19th century. Many famous former residents had Royal connections but the School was only established in 1923 and is a relative newcomer when compared with other schools in this publication. Now home to 630 pupils, 257 girls and 373 boys of whom two thirds board, Canford School is the undiscovered jewel of the South.

Opulent in its setting but unpretentious in its achievements, the school has been climbing league tables quietly but steadily. It is now listed at number 175 in the 2011 FT Top 1000 Schools (all schools not just independent) comparing very favourably with neighbours like Bryanstone (450) and Sherborne (316). Yet Canford is not one of the famous names that roll of the tongue when talking of public boarding schools yet outperforms many of those that do. Headmaster John Lever is happy with that. Many schools are hampered by their heritage and are led by a board stuffed with multiple generations of old boys who quote how it used to be and what school mores dictate. Not so Canford, it is relatively young and its Headmaster does not feel encumbered by stuffy traditions that could get in the way of the pursuit of excellence. In a discussion with the parents of a particularly gifted boy, Lever was reported to respond to their stellar academic aspirations with the comment: "I think it is more important that your son can hold an interesting dinner conversation". They did not send their son to Canford and the school is probably a better place for it. Does that mean that Canford is not for the academically gifted? It is just that but along the way also develops grounded and well-rounded young people, equipped to contribute positively to society.

The 2012 Independent Schools Inspectorate report supports these aspirations fully with pages peppered with superlatives and no criticism of any substance of either the education or pastoral care. The list of sporting, outdoor as well as charity activities mounted from the school is impressive. The school focuses on rugby, hockey, cricket and netball but lacrosse also features; the school has ample playing fields and courts to accommodate a comprehensive range of sports. The well- equipped boathouse with professional coaching staff ensures that Canford regularly features as one of the top rowing schools regularly delivering candidates for team GB.

Headmaster John Lever is clear about his aims and where he sees his market. The school does not particularly court the rich and famous and they prefer parents who work hard for the money they spend on their children's education. It makes for more appreciative and hard working students. The school has a rich mixture of parents rather than a mixture of rich parents and seems not to be dominated by the London set; here it is possible to find parents who are not hedge fund managers. The school rarely advertises; it does not need to. Canford's results and the parents' network keep the school's admission list full for years ahead. Accordingly, admission needs to be applied for in good time. In common with many schools, Canford seeks to gain commitment from parents with a sizable down payment a year ahead of common entrance exams.

Academically less selective than many other high performing schools, which in turn makes Canford's achievements all the greater. The added value this school delivers is very significant. It achieves this by emphasising personal responsibility. Discipline is clear and firm but low key and largely self-regulating as respect, self-discipline and maturity of behaviour are encouraged throughout the school. There is a system of prefects in each of the houses who administer aspects like time keeping and roll calls but again a light touch seems to pervade. The standards are clearly set and compliance is expected and delivered rather than enforced. The head girl and boy are appointed and their duties are similarly understated and largely representative.

Most people reading this will be looking for advice on where to send their offspring. Many will be bewildered by the choice and this book should help narrow the choice and offer a route to final selection. My advice is simple: the short list can be developed with one's head but the final selection is very much a matter for the heart. There is no better way than to walk the school grounds and carefully to observe the pupils as they interact with you, with their teachers and, most important of all, with each other. The question to ask yourself is this: do I want my children to be like these youngsters? In the early years parental influence is greatest; in the teenage years peer influence is greater yet, especially at boarding school. The people you observe during the open day will have an inordinate impact on how your little darling will grow up.

At Canford we found a vigorous, robust atmosphere of hard work, hard play but also one of mutual support and courtesy. Having picked the school, the next major decision not to be taken lightly is the choice of house or more accurately the house master/mistress. This person will interact daily and have a significant influence over every aspect of junior's life at the school. You will also interact regularly and there needs to be synergy for this relationship to work. Chose accordingly.

Now in the third year of being a Canford parent I have been supremely impressed with the work ethic of the school and with the way the teachers have extracted every bit of academic and sporting potential out of my son and his fellows. Long may they continue to do so! John Lever is set to depart the school in the near future but he leaves a rock solid legacy and some big shoes to fill. His replacement must be selected very carefully to ensure the continued success of this gem.

John Bleeker is a wing commander in the Royal Air Force who with his wife Susie, a National Health Service hospital director, lives in the Test Valley in Hampshire. They have a son at Canford and, thinking specifically academic, single-sex education more suited to their daughter, sent her to St Mary's School in Ascot.

CHARTERHOUSE

Godalming

Surrey GU7 2DX

www.charterhouse.org.uk

01483 291501

THIS grand old school was founded in London in 1611, but moved to its present site near Godalming in 1872, where it occupies 250 acres of pleasant Surrey countryside. The schools' stunning buildings are conveniently located only 45 minutes from London and within easy reach of Gatwick and Heathrow airports. Charterhouse was one of the original 9 public schools as defined by the Public Schools Act of 1868 which derived from the Clarendon Commission of 1864. The Act was enacted to regulate and reform the nine leading boys' schools of that era and in addition to Charterhouse it included Eton, Harrow, Winchester, Westminster, Rugby, Shrewsbury, St Paul's and Merchant Taylors'.

With 400 years of history to celebrate, Charterhouse remains predominantly a single sex boarding school where only a handful of day pupils are admitted. Girls are only accepted into the Sixth Form at 16+ which means that one must view this school as a full boarding educational establishment where boys easily outnumber girls. One can register a boy at any time after birth, but at the very latest three years before the proposed entry. Two years prior to starting at Charterhouse a report will be requested from the boy's current prep school and so long as this is satisfactory, a place will be offered subject to a pass in the Common Entrance Examination acceptable to the school. Unlike Eton, Harrow, Wellington and a few others, there is no "stressful" pre-testing at

Charterhouse. There are now 770 pupils at the school (84% boys, 16% girls) and the fees are staggeringly high at £29,400 for boarders and £ 24,300 for day boarders. A new Sixth Form Day House for 50 boys and girls has recently been opened to complement the existing eleven boarding Houses which have all preserved their own identity and each have their own tie and colours. Boys come from a wide selection of prep schools including many from London and the South East. Approximately 18% of the pupils come from abroad with Chinese and Russians making up a fair number.

Once upon a time Charterhouse was fairly "Old Money" and a significant number of boys would come from a wide geographical area stretching well beyond the Home Counties. Apparently, this is no longer thought to be the case. Nowadays, although some pupils do come from distant parts, the schools' catchment area is considerably more parochial with large numbers coming from West and South London, Surrey, East Berkshire, Kent and Sussex. In other words, close enough for mummy and daddy to bomb over for games, concerts etc. in less than an hour. What this means of course, is that modern day Charterhouse has a much more metropolitan feel to it and the hunting, shooting and fishing types from the Shires are less prevalent than they once were. This was made unequivocally clear to me by a senior master from Charterhouse. Apparently, a large number of boys from Eton, Radley and even Harrow attended the march in London in 2002, to protest against the Labour Government proposed bill to ban hunting with dogs. However, as far as he could recall only a handful of Carthusians chose to make the trip to the capital and stand up for rural sports. It was Oscar Wilde (not a Carthusian), who described Fox Hunters as the "unspeakable in pursuit of the uneatable", but clearly, many of the boys and girls at Charterhouse prefer to spend their leisure time pursuing activities which may not involve catching salmon or shooting game let alone chasing vermin on a horseback.

Moving on to more important matters, the fact that the schools social image may no longer be one of Land Rovers and Labradors, is largely irrelevant. Most parents who are interested in this school are probably more focused on what it has to offer educationally and pastorally rather than socially. With this in mind, I would like to quote from a passage written by the present Headmaster, The Reverend John Witheridge. This is what he has to say about Charterhouse: "We seek to ensure that, by the time they leave us, our boys and girls are so highly qualified that they pass into the best universities, in Britain and abroad; however, our priority is not examination grades but the stimulation of independent enquiry and intellectual curiosity". So they you have it; a school that will strive to get your child into the best university possible whilst ensuring that he or she also acquires the knowledge and social skills essential for survival in the competitive world we now live in.

So how academic is this school compared to some of its competitors? In 2011, the highly respected Financial Times Academic Tables for Independent Schools placed Charterhouse in 84th place, which is most commendable for a school that does not have a highly selective admission policy. Admittedly, this is not as good as Tonbridge 9th, Radley 23rd and Harrow 39th. However, the Oxbridge/UCL success rate at 15% is undeniably impressive and almost as good as Harrow 17%, Radley 17% and certainly better than Wellington 9%. Last year 13 pupils won places at Oxford and 7 went to Cambridge. Charterhouse may not be an academic hot house, but, it is hardly a place for slackers or unmotivated characters. Whether the adoption of the more intellectually rigorous Cambridge Pre-U as well as the introduction of the I.B. will raise the academic bar at this school remains to be seen. Please watch this space. However, the signs are good and many believe that academically this educational establishment is steadily heading north and most definitely deserves its reputation as a top drawer public school.

There is no serious rugby at this school and the main winter sport is football. Perhaps this explains why the former England international Garry Lineker chose to send his son here. In fact Charterhouse can historically claim to have jointly founded the game of football with Westminster School and not surprisingly these two famous schools continue to excel in the sport. During the last few years, Charterhouse has performed admirably in the Independent Schools Association Football cup, winning the trophy in 2008 by beating Millfield and another success in 2010 with a victory in the final over Eton. However, the fact that rugby enjoys a low profile at this school does deter some families. Many traditionalists still feel that rugby and public schools go hand in hand and will steer clear of schools that do not take the game seriously. Cricket on the other hand is well established and the school has produced many first-class cricketers, none more famous than Peter May. The cricket pitch is located against the spectacular backdrop of school and chapel. In general, the sporting facilities at Charterhouse are very impressive and include the Queen's Sports Centre with its indoor swimming pool, climbing wall and fitness suite. The school also has a nine hole golf course and all weather pitches used for tennis and hockey.

Charterhouse is a school with a strong Christian tradition which still expresses itself in regular worship. By 1914 the original chapel was no longer large enough to accommodate the growing number of boys so Memorial Chapel designed by Sir Giles Gilbert Scott, perhaps more famous for the red telephone box, was built. Memorial Chapel consecrated in 1927 commemorates the many Carthusians who died in the two World Wars and the school meets here five days per week at 8.30 in the morning for a short service and on Sundays for evensong. Parents are welcome to Sunday services but tickets are required for popular events like Carol Services or Remembrance Sunday.

Like most traditional public schools, pupils at Charterhouse wear smart uniforms which most parents find attractive and reassuring. The Lower School which consists of the first three years sees boys attired in white shirts, grey trousers, House ties, blue jumpers and tweed jackets finished off with leather shoes. On Sundays these "Lower" boys School Dress consists of a dark plain or pinstriped suits. The so called Specialists, pupils in the Sixth Form, have their own variations on School Dress and tend to wear navy blazers instead of tweed jackets. During the Cricket Quarter boys may wear cravats instead of ties and pupils in the Lower School may also wear navy blazers instead of tweed jackets. Furthermore, during the Cricket Quarter, boys may wear a straw Boater similar to the Harrow hat worn by Harrovians throughout the academic year. However, I believe that very few boys at Charterhouse chose to wear the straw hat!

On leaving Charterhouse, most Carthusians tend to end up at the usual "Rah Unis" such as Bristol, Durham, Edinburgh, UCL, Leeds, Nottingham, Exeter and Oxbridge where they generally tend to socialise with other public schools educated students. Understandably, not everyone likes the sound of "cut glass" accents reverberating loudly throughout our so called elite universities, least of all, left leaning commentators who argue that schools like Charterhouse are over-represented at these institutions. Top universities, those perceived to be the preserve of the privately educated middle classes, are now under immense political pressure to widen access or risk losing out financially. This argument is all well and good, but clearly it fails to take into account the simple fact that humans will always feel more comfortable in the company of likeminded individuals and no amount of social engineering will ever change that. University students from the other side of the social divide may be inclined to label Carthhusians as "Toffs" but, from what I have heard they are generally well mannered , good social mixers and most definitely not arrogant. On the whole they are respected and admired, but do not quite enjoy the same lofty social standing at university as Etonians.

Charterhouse is a traditional and yet progressive school with a strong boarding ethos. The school is academically sound and achieves very good examination results as well as turning out confident and rounded individuals. Over the years the school has educated a large number of distinguished men such as the Novelist William Thackeray, Politician and Journalist William Rees-Mogg, Television Presenter David Dimbleby, Radio and Television Presenter Jonathan Dimbleby, Music Impressario Jonathan King, the Cricketer Peter May, Businessman Archie Norman, Tory Politician and Secretary of State Jeremy Hunt, Journalist and Author Max Hastings and the founding members of the 1970's Rock Band Genesis

In summary a well known educational establishment that retains many of the cherished characteristics of the classic English public school. Academic results exceed expectations and the majority progress to first rate universities. This is a forward looking school with a healthy social and ethnic mix. Anyone residing within a reasonable distance from this school should give it serious consideration.

CHELTENHAM LADIES COLLEGE

Bayshill Road

Cheltenahm GL50 3EP

www.cheltladiescollege.org

01242 520691

CHELTENHAM Ladies College has had a shot of adrenaline following the appointment of Eve Jardine-Young as Headmistress in September 2011. Ms Jardine-Young is an old girl of the College and has a very impressive pedigree with stints teaching at Radley, Epsom College and most recently Director of Studies at Blundell. However following in the footsteps of Vicky Tuck this school has never been without a very strong woman at the helm. In fact one of the greatest strengths of a girls only school is the can do attitude which is fostered in all pupils. Girls lead and they know no different.

Established in 1853 the school is set in the beautiful Regency town of Cheltenham with many girls coming from Gloucestershire but a fair number from the rest of the United Kingdom and indeed around the world as you would expect for a school of this calibre. Girls have joined the school from over 400 different preps. As the largest girls' boarding school in Europe, this is an attraction for many. Of the 855 girls around 75% are boarders, split among 10 houses with an additional four day houses. Interestingly the boarding houses are separated into four senior houses for Sixth Formers and six junior houses for girls aged 11 to 16. This division of age groups is held throughout the school with girls in years 7-9 making up Lower College, then moving on to Upper College and finally Sixth Form.

It's wise to register your daughter two years before proposed entry and girls may join the school aged 11+, 12+ or 13+. There are very few places available for sixth form entry. Fees are predictably high, full boarding will set you back around £10,800 per term but financial assistance is possible made even more so by the fact that 2% of all fees go to a bursaries fund. There is also a raft of scholarships for girls who excel academically or in art, music or sport which usually cover 15% of the fees. The latest of these is The Vicky Tuck Scholarship, after 15 years as headmistress her legacy could never be boiled down to just a scholarship and this is a interesting one in that it goes to a Sixth Form girl with part of the scholarship including an international work placement.

Academically CLC plays in the big leagues with 26% of girls obtaining a place at Oxford or Cambridge and they were ranked 34th on last year's Financial Times Independent Schools table. Not quite as highly as Wycombe Abbey (2nd) or St Pauls Girls' (6th) but streets ahead of Roedean (158), Benenden (104) and Downe House (123). As one would expect sport, drama, art and music are not neglected. The music department proudly notes that 800 individual music lessons are given each week without a girl missing an academic lesson. Quite an extraordinary feat of timetable management! Over 30 sports are offered, from polo to trampolining and the school has amongst its facilities 17 netball courts, 24 tennis courts and an ozone (chlorine free) swimming pool. Clubs and activities abound so you can be sure your daughter would never be unfit or bored. In 2009 College opened the Parabola Arts Centre which houses an award winning theatre. Several performances are put on annually and success has been achieved at the Edinburgh Fringe Festival.

The list of old girls is impressive in its diversity from actresses such as Kristin Scott Thomas to fashion designers Amanda Wakeley and Katherine Hamnett to high flying financier Nicola Horlick and the Deputy Governor of the Bank of England, Rachel Lomax and current

Cabinet Minister Cheryl Gillan. As my mother in law is herself an old girl, had my wife and I had daughters we would most certainly have considered this school very highly. A comment from the schools website perfectly sums up the ethos of Cheltenham Ladies College: "An education for a life beyond school". It certainly does exactly that.

Mario di Monaco and Kerry Rhodes

DOWNE HOUSE SCHOOL

Cold Ash

Berkshire RG18 9JJ

www.downehouse.net

01635 200286

DOWNE House is everything that you would expect from a girls boarding school but then so very much more. Probably its most unique selling point is that every girl in their second year will spend an entire term at Veyrines-de-Domme, a satellite of Down House located in Perigord Noir in the Dordogne region of France. Certainly a change of scenery from Cold Ash in Berkshire! With all lessons, bar English of course, being taught in French pupils are completely immersed in the language and culture surrounding them. Aside from all normal lessons weekly sorties to the theatre or concerts as well as visits to see an "artisan chocolatier" or jewellery maker at work are planned.

Girls join Downe House at age 11 and some 95% board. Accommodated in one of the eight Houses pastoral care is very good with the usual staff of House Mistress, matrons and tutors but by the Sixth Form every girl has her own individually assigned personal tutor. A resource and support which is extremely highly valued by girls and parents alike when faced with the process of university applications or discussions on the possibilities of a gap year.

The academic standards at Downe House are rigorous and in 2010 the Cambridge Pre-U was introduced as the school felt that some A Level course were not challenging enough. However, the results of the 2011 A-

Levels were very good with 65.7% of girls obtaining A*A grades. Other than the 15% of pupils who are offered places at Cambridge or Oxford, the majority of leavers headed for Manchester, Durham, Newcastle, Bristol or Exeter with just a smattering going to the famous London universities such as UCL or Imperial. This is a very well rounded school with great emphasis placed on the arts. Drama and music are catered for with wonderful facilities. As is sport with PE being a compulsory part of the curriculum and if that doesn't appeal there is every sport from lacrosse, tennis or swimming to the somewhat unusual for a rather elite girls school - touch rugby! In a boarding environment there really is so much more time to spread out lessons and activities throughout the weekend as well giving girls the opportunity to enjoy the many clubs on offer which range from a politics society and mock United Nations to a number of orchestras and music ensembles as well as choirs, jewellery making or a science club. The Duke of Edinburgh awards scheme is run in conjunction with other local senior schools which is a great way of promoting interaction within the community. In fact Downe House quite rightly prides itself on these community links which also include offering mock Oxbridge interviews to local pupils, members of staff teaching lessons in some local schools and the girls own efforts in fundraising and helping at a nearby Riding for the Disabled centre.

When Olive Willis, the school's first headmistress, founded Downe House in 1907 she believed that "excellence, excitement and enthusiasm for the world around should be the hallmarks of a school community". This ethos still holds true today.

The comments below are from a current pupil and parent and gives a first hand account of life at Downe House;

Downe House – January 2012

Downe House is an independent boarding school for girls aged 11 to 18. It is situated just outside Newbury with over 110 acres.

It is a wonderful experience and even in one year I have learnt so much.

In Removes (year 8) there are two houses, Hill and Hermitage. I was in Hill which is a short walk into the main school. Now back from France I am in Darwin House which is for the Lower Fours. For the following three years you will stay in your school house – I am Asholt. The sixth form have their own houses.

My headmistress Mrs McKendrick is really kind and encouraging and helps everyone until the end. She knows everyone's names and gives them all a birthday card. All of the teachers are so motivating and helpful, Downe House's aim is to make sure everyone knows what they are good at and make sure they use that in later life. The careers department offer so much advice and choice. You can use the library whenever you need to and there are so many books to choose from.

Downe House is well known for its sport, music, drama and art. We recently performed Alice in Wonderland which was fantastic. There are so many new activities and hobbies to try. I have started squash and the trumpet. I have also tried pottery. But I still play tennis, the piano and dance. Also I am in the swimming team. Every Tuesday we have Junior chapel in the morning. There is a Junior and Senior choir. We sometimes give performances in chapel and in March 2012 we will visit Venice to sing there.

I have just been to spend a term in France at the Downe House School in Veyrine. Everyone in Year 8 (Lower 4) spends one term there.

It was an amazing experience, I enjoyed every second and learnt so much about myself (and my French improved!) All the subjects were taught in French (apart from Maths and English) so my French improved quickly. Nearly every day we went on sorties, such as truffle hunting, visiting caves, cooking and the two main trips to Vulcania and Futuroscope were so much fun and I learnt a great deal from them. It is situated in the Dordogne region and it is called Veyrines de Dome. It is a tiny village so you get to know everyone very quickly. The Head of France is Mrs Gwatkins and she is very kind. There is also Mr Gwatkins and their dog, Mr Green. They believe in trust, freedom and responsibility.

Although boarding seemed scary at the start and I missed home a lot. Hill house was a great place with loads to do and lots of friends. Every weekend is filled with activities and sport so no one can get lonely or bored. Soon I found when at home I missed school!

Downe House – a parents perspective

We chose Downe House for its academic achievements but also its pastoral care, which we knew would meet our daughter's needs. The level of pastoral care is very high with the house mistresses able to help the girls with any problems or worries they might have.

We had not planned on full boarding but realised that with two other children flexi boarding would not work as we would be unable to pick her up when she wanted to come home mid week. Also flexi boarding seemed to offer little at weekends because most children went home. Our daughter joined at 11 years old and had no previous boarding experience but after a few wobbly days settled in and has never looked back. The school keep the girls in Remove and Lower Four (yrs 7 and 8) in separate houses. It allows the girls to get to know each other and not worry about the older girls. In Upper Four (yr9) they join their school houses which sleep Upper Four to Upper Five.

In Lower Four the girls spend a term at Downe House's school in France in the Dordogne. It is an amazing experience. Although a great deal of fun they learn so much, not only the French language. It is a great shame that due to the amount of academic learning in the older years they do not have time to visit again.

Downe House has a very full term of sport, activities, entertainment – so much that she does not always come home for her floating exeats as there is too much she will miss out on!

ETON COLLEGE

Windsor

Berkshire SL4 6DB

www.etoncollege.com

01753 671249

PRINCE William's Alma Mater is undeniably the most famous school in the English speaking world. For centuries this place has been a magnet for ambitious boys from every corner of Britain as well as abroad. The school has been so hugely successful that it would be hard to overstate its influence on the institutions of power and is overrepresentation in many areas of our national life. So far a staggering 19 British Prime Ministers have attended this superb educational establishment including our present leader David Cameron.

Founded in 1440 by Henry VI, Eton's imposing buildings are situated a stone's throw from Windsor Castle on the other side of the river Thames. Although Eton has made great progress in attracting boys from diverse backgrounds, there are still many people in Britain who would love to see this school razed to the ground. In an egalitarian society they argue, there is no place for elite private schools of this nature churning out privileged and arrogant young men. This of course is a simplistic one sided view that fails to look at the complete picture. Most Etonians although privileged, are also polite, talented, creative, considerate, discreet and unassuming. Naturally, there will always be some who get carried away with their own self importance and let the side down. A classic example of Etonians behaving foolishly was recently witnessed during a football match against Charterhouse. Apparently a group of boys from the school taunted the opposition with chants of "19 Prime Ministers and one day you will work for us"!

Moving on to more pressing issues, what seems to preoccupy the vast majority of prospective parents is how to crack the reputedly difficult entrance assessment. Once upon a time if your father had attended this school, in all probability you would have been ushered in on the nod. Your parents had to simply drop a line to a friendly Housemaster who would register you on his list and so long as you obtained a satisfactory pass in Common Entrance you were home and dry. Those were the days when up to 70% of the boys at Eton had family connections to the school. This is definitely no longer the case and most parents would do well to realise that the image of Eton as a school for the sons of the Aristocracy, the landed gentry and the fabulously rich is now old hat.

Nowadays a more modest 40% of the boys have a family connection to Eton and there is definitely a more international feel to the place. Apparently contemporary Etonians hail from 40 different countries. Furthermore, up to a fifth of the boys at Eton receive significant financial assistance from the school and according to the Headmaster ambitious plans are being developed for Eton to go completely "needs blind" in the future. The objective is to allow any boy to attend this famous school irrespective of their parents' ability to pay. Clearly the success of this system is limited by the amount of money in the schools bursary pot.

The changes in the social makeup of the school have largely come about as a result of the new admission policy which now focuses a great deal more on overall abilities and less on historical ties to Eton. Not surprisingly this has not been universally popular. Traditional Etonian families who have attended this school for generations feel particularly aggrieved if their sons fail to make the cut and are politely advised to look elsewhere. One can sympathise with their predicament but, the world has moved on and Eton is no longer the "Slough comprehensive" of old. These days the academically challenged, irrespective of background, would be hard pressed to survive the thrilling but intensive journey. As one Etonian parent recently told me: modern day Eton is like boarding a 90 mile per hour train packed with multitalented and competitive boys.

So what exactly is the Eton entrance assessment and how can one prepare for it? Firstly it is important to realise that according to Anthony Little, the present Headmaster, contemporary Etonians are not all "academic superstars". Apparently the school is less selective than Winchester, Westminster or St Pauls. When we last spoke the Headmaster made it quite clear that although the ideal Etonian needs to be academically comfortable he also needs to possess resilience and bring something else to the party other than just good exam results. If a boy is clever but dull, he may be directed towards another more suitable school. The present admission system requires would-be Etonians to be registered on the "Eton List" by the age of 10 ½ and then go through a selection procedure at about 11. Competition for the 250 places available annually is fierce, with approximately 1,000 boys travelling to Eton to sit the assessment. There are three equal parts to it.

- An interview

- A report from their prep school headmaster.

- A computerised formal test, specially designed for Eton, to test reasoning ability.

Of the three components which make up the selection procedure, the computerised test is the one that tends to cause the most anxiety. This is understandable, but the school has been known to reject boys who scored well in the computer test but failed to impress in other parts of the assessment. Boys who successfully overcome these three hurdles will be offered conditional places, subject to their passing the subsequent Common Entrance Examination to a standard acceptable to Eton, currently set at a minimum of 65%. Last year (2010) the Eton Common Entrance average pass mark was 70% with only 0.3% failing the examination.

The much talked about computer test used by Eton to gauge reasoning ability has become almost legendary. This test which lasts 80 minutes, with each question being "timed out" has been designed to assess one's innate ability and therefore it is almost impossible to prepare for. It is also a level playing field which means that boys who attended expensive academic prep schools do not have the upper hand. In theory a capable boy from a state junior school stands as much chance of success as a boy from Ludgrove or Summer Fields. Interestingly, I once sat next to a lady whose son was at Eton who told me that in her view the best way to prepare for the computer test was to allow one's son to spend a great deal of time on his Play Station!

Following the entrance assessment 250 offers are made yearly and approximately 50 other boys are placed on a graded waiting list. The remaining 700 or so who have not been offered anything will be advised to look elsewhere. Clearly, the vast majority of prospective Etonians are destined to fall at the first hurdle and many will end up at places which their parents feel are suitable alternatives. This has given rise to a group of socially acceptable schools described by some as the "Eton Diaspora" which is known to include Harrow, Radley, Stowe, Marlborough, Shrewsbury, Rugby and one or two others.

A recent drive to recruit new blood has seen the number of prep schools sending boys to Eton increase from 50, ten years ago, to 94 in 2010. Having said that, "traditional feeders" such as Ludgrove and Summer Fields respectively sent 16 and 15 boys to Eton in 2011. It is also worth noting that 90% of the boys at Eton come from British prep schools and 10% from abroad including expats. Furthermore, contemporary Etonians who have attended boarding preps make up a smaller number than was the case a decade or so ago, probably because nowadays more boys come from academic London day schools.

Eton College is one of the largest public schools in Britain with 1300 pupils. The boys are accommodated in one of the 24 boarding houses scattered throughout the town, which have an average of 50 boys in each. Every boy has his own study-bedroom from the start. Each house is under the control of a Housemaster and a Dame together with an assistant tutor. The 70 Kings Scholars are accommodated in the splendid medieval building known as College. These Collegers or "Tugs" are distinguished by their black gowns and attend Eton on scholarships awarded by competitive examination. These scholarships are now worth on average 10% of the full fees, considerably less than the 50% that had traditionally been the case not so long ago. Means tested bursaries are available to help bright boys from poorer homes attend Eton and four years ago the school announced plans to raise £50 million designed to finance and expand the bursary pot.

Unlike Westminster or St Pauls which are still widely regarded as academic powerhouses, Eton likes to portray itself as a more rounded school with a diverse intake. That said, Eton's academic results have improved substantially over the last ten years or so and are now quite outstanding. According to The Sunday Times 2010 examination results listing the top 100 independent schools, Eton College was ranked 12[th.] The percentage of A*-B grades at A-Level was 96.2% and GCSE results A*-A grades came in at 97.7%. Of its competitors only St Pauls School (2) and Westminster (7) were ranked higher. However, Eton did better than Harrow (35), Radley (57), Oundle (58), Rugby (82), Wellington College (83) and Marlborough (87). Eton of course need not concern itself with academic rivalry or league tables. The high profile nature of the school coupled with its very special "brand" speaks for itself. Also impressive is Eton's ability to ship boys into top universities both in the U.K. and America. The Oxbridge "hit rate" stands at an enviable 35% with Oxford being more popular than Cambridge. The rest disperse to highly respected Russell group universities such as Bristol, Edinburgh, U.C.L. Imperial College etc. and some go to less academic but equally "Rah" institutions such as Durham, Newcastle, St Andrews or Exeter. An increasing number who fail to win Oxbridge places are shunning less renowned British universities and opting for American Ivy League Colleges such as Harvard, Yale or Princeton.

The Duke of Wellington, who attended Eton in the late 18th century, is often quoted as saying that "the Battle of Waterloo was won on the playing fields of Eton". This is probably untrue as in his days at Eton, there were no playing fields or organised team sports. Thankfully, Eton now has acres of playing fields and fantastic facilities to cater for most sporting activities including a lake which will be the venue for the rowing events at the 2012 London Olympics. Whilst on the subject of rowing, the "wet bobs" have had great success at Henley of late and the school has lifted the Princes Elizabeth cup twice in the last three years. Rowing is still close to Etonians' hearts and the Eton Boating Song remains one of the best known of the genre:

Jolly boating weather,
And a hay harvest breeze,
Blade on the feather,
Shade of the trees,
Swing, swing together
With your bodies between your knees.

Success in rowing however has not necessarily been replicated in other traditional public schools sports. To the disappointment of many Etonians, last year Radley, a school with only 690 boys managed to beat Eton both at rugby and cricket. Even more disappointing was losing the annual cricket match at Lord's against their sporting rivals Harrow in 2010. However, a strong Eton side gained revenge in 2011 by comfortably outscoring Harrow. This traditional fixture between the two most famous English schools is one of the oldest in the cricketing calendar having been contested since 1805 when the poet Lord Byron batted for the losing Harrow side. Football on the other hand has become popular at Eton and the school has had some notable success in this sport. Generally speaking, Eton is a strong sporting school where almost any activity is possible.

21st Century Eton may no longer be the bastion of aristocratic privilege it once was, but many old traditions continue in a timeless fashion. The school remains boys only and full boarding with no plans to admit girls or introduce day places. Flexi-boarding which has become popular at some traditional boarding schools is not on the cards either. Furthermore, the boys still wear the famous uniform which consists of tailcoat, waistcoat and white tie. Apparently this uniform is extremely practical and the boys, irrespective of social background, love wearing it. Whilst on the subject of uniforms, members of the schools prefectorial body, known as "Pop", are entitled to wear something flashier and can be distinguished by their colourful waistcoats and spongebag trousers. Since its foundation in 1811 "Pop" has largely retained its self-elected membership. Naturally, those who are elected to this exclusive group feel rather cool. On the other hand parents of boys who have not been elected have been known to create a bit of a stir.

Eton, of course, is not just an academic school with an impeccable pedigree. So much of what is on offer here is of the highest quality and the boys are all encouraged to tap into the fantastic resources which are available. The reputation of the teaching staff is excellent and its members have been recruited from fields as diverse as banking, law and the army as well as the world of academia. Social interaction between boys, Housemasters and tutors is actively promoted and pupils learn from an early age how to hold their own in a competitive environment. When it comes to nurturing inherent abilities, Eton, does it better than most other schools and it is hardly surprising that so many boys emerge from this school with a multitude of talents. A word of caution, however, Eton is not a place for boys who prefer to be spoon fed or taught in a didactic "talk and chalk" way. This school is best suited to self motivated and reflective boys who can think on their feet.

On the 28th April 2011, the eve of the Royal Wedding of HRH Prince William and Miss Catherine Middleton my wife and I visited Eton as we had an appointment with the Headmaster, Anthony Little, to pick his brain over coffee. As we walked along the hallway towards his office we encountered the famous oil painting of Princes William and Harry looking young and fresh-faced. Of course, unlike their father who was schooled at Gordonstoun in Scotland, the Princes were educated at Eton. We were hugely grateful to be granted nearly two hours of Mr Little's precious time and we thoroughly enjoyed the stimulating dialogue that took place. The headmaster, an erudite Old Etonian, is most definitely a great asset to this school. We found his effortless and understated charm infectious and could have easily spent the whole day in his company.

My thoughts on Eton by Sandy Loder and Robert Loder

As an old Etonian going back to one's old school, it was surprising to see quite a few fellow old Etonians. The perk of going to Eton is the incredible alumni that one joins. It is an amazing club that has a huge global membership in all sectors of business and in all countries around the world. For instance, I was in the same class as the current British Prime Minister and at Eton at the same time as the Mayor of London and Jay Jopling of White Cube.

I have been very impressed by the briefings and visits to the school prior to my son joining. Despite the large size of the school, the houses where the boys board are quite small and the pastoral care for the boys is phenomenal. There is an amazing attention to detail for each individual especially from the Housemasters. Compared to prep school, you have to have faith in the school and its system as you only get one parent/teacher meeting in the year. However, there is constant feedback from the Housemaster.

It is very much like a university and the boys are very much left to their own devices to plan their homework, so they need to develop some semblance of self discipline instead of playing games on the computer! They are very much treated like adults and are expected to deliver the work. This type of learning can take time to adjust to initially. Overall the school has a very good atmosphere, is friendly and despite its size does everything to make one feel welcome and wanted.

A natural competitiveness evolves as there are over 250 boys in every year competing for limited spaces in first teams at sport for instance. Not a bad life skill to pick up early in life.

The school seems more relaxed and friendlier than in the early 1980s. Beatings have stopped and teachers are very much using first names to address boys. The facilities available to the boys are incredible both in sport, music and art. There is a constant programme of building improvements.

The school has a high academic standard which is taken as a "given" by the boys. The kudos comes from being in a sports team or extra-curricular activity such as art or music. There are many more children of professionals from all over the world now than 30 years ago. Overall, I would say that the school very much reflects modern Britain and is very multi-cultural.

As an old Etonian, you always think the Eton is the best and therefore do not need to take your son to see other schools. It was very interesting when my wife arranged for us to go and see about half a dozen other schools. All had their positive and negative points, but what stood out was the spectacular facilities provided by Eton. From the standard of teaching to the incredible range of sporting opportunities. This latter point is reflected in Dorney Lake, a venue for the London 2012 Olympics rowing but also how many pupils represent Great Britain in that sport.

The downside to the school is the size and no co-education, but you cannot have everything. Finally, the school has an inspiring headmaster, who brings intellect, humour and a fresh view on academic teaching.

A view from Robert Loder – a current pupil

Upon arriving at the school it was not what I initially expected, but in a good way, Eton College is a beautiful and wonderful place, once you get to know the people in your house. From playing football after supper to

Trials in the Whitely Hall, my first year of at Eton College has been the most exciting year of my life where I have learnt many valuable lessons, not just how to improve in algebra, but how competitive life really can be. I personally learnt this in the soccer trials of Michaelmas where I didn't make it into a team but managed to make it into a rugby team by the end having to grit my teeth and become more determined. This school is not for slackers who aim to get by because they just don't last at this school, most people aim to be the best.

In conclusion, people think that Eton is mostly academic but this is not the case, in fact the academic side of things is probably the least biggest factor which a boy at Eton has to deal with and if you try your hardest and just be yourself you will be fine because everybody is different in their own ways, from being a footballer on the AstroTurf to being in the chess club. This school has the widest range of people from all over the world and yes some people may have more friends but, you will find a friend without a doubt.

FETTES COLLEGE

Carrington Road

Edinburgh EH4 1QX

www.fettes.com

0131 3116744

THIS grand school is located in the Scottish capital Edinburgh, and was established by Sir William Fettes in 1870. The school buildings are truly spectacular and bear a striking resemblance to Hogwarts, the fictional School of Magic and Wizardry attended by the young wizard Harry Potter and his friends. Photographs of Fettes in the snow are particularly enchanting and one can only envy the boys and girls who spend five glorious years of their lives in such a beautiful environment. The school occupies a 100 acres site a short ten minutes walk from the city centre. The ex -Prime Minister Tony Blair was educated at Fettes and during his time at 10 Downing Street the school enjoyed a prolonged period of media attention. Whether or not this school and not Ampleforth or Glenalmond is the true "Eton of the North" is purely academic. However, rather interestingly, the impeccably mannered James Bond (007) created by Ian Fleming's and immortalised in many films, is supposed to have attended Fettes after having been removed from Eton!

Fettes is a leading co-educational boarding and day school that can justifiable claim to be one of the best in Scotland. Academic results are impressive and the school enjoys a high social standing not just in Scotland, but throughout Britain. There are approximately 700 pupils at Fettes and 80% are boarders. Most of the day students come from Edinburgh and the affluent communities within easy reach of the capital.

103

Girls make up 45% of the schools intake at present, and boarding fees are £26,000 per annum, much the same as Glenalmond College and Loretto. However, there is a reduction in fees for siblings depending on the number of children from the same family attending the school. Please contact the school for further details of this important scheme. Pupils from overseas account for some 12% of the schools total and come from 40 different nations.

There are eight boarding Houses in total, four for boys, three for girls and one mixed for the upper Sixth Form. The Houses are well run by a Housemaster/mistress as well as a resident tutor and matron, who together ensure that the pastoral care at Fettes is second to none. As Houses fill up two years ahead of entry it's a good idea to register early so as not to be disappointed. At 13+ the procedure is fairly standard, interviews and Common Entrance Examination or Fettes Entrance Examination. A number of scholarships are also available and include: academic, music, sport, all-round, piping and art. Scholarship holders are entitled to a reduction in fees of up to 10% and mean tested bursaries that can cover up to 105% of the fees. At 16+ (entry into the Sixth Form), applicants are expected to have at least six GCSEs passes with B grades of higher.

Academic results are good and candidates can choose to study for the broader I.B. or stick to the traditional A-levels. Fettes usually obtains some of the best academic results in Scotland and in 2011 the students who sat the I.B. obtained an average score of 36.2 which is highly commendable. A-level results were good if not spectacular, with the A*A and B pass rate coming in at a satisfactory 76%. Whilst these results compare reasonably well with many other public schools, I would not categorise Fettes as an overly academic school. A total of 8 pupils won places at Oxford or Cambridge which is somewhat lower than previous years. This is possibly the result of Government pressure on elite universities to widen access and admit more boys and girls from the State sector. Many British public schools of the academic broad church variety have seen their Oxbridge hit rate reduced unlike the academic hot houses which, if anything, seem to be tightening their grip on our two most famous universities. One need not despair however, academic excellence does not stop at Oxbridge and the vast majority of Fettes pupils go on to good universities with Edinburgh, Bristol and St Andrews being popular destinations.

All the usual sports are on offer and rugby is played to a high standard. Fettes has produced 60 international rugby players over the years and I dare say it will continue to do so for years to come. The Scottish national side that sadly picked up the wooden spoon in this year's Six Nations Rugby Tournament, could most certainly do with some new blood from this great public school. Girls have been particularly successful in lacrosse and hockey and the school have a good fencing team. There is also canoeing and climbing in the Scottish mountains and the Duke of Edinburgh Awards is very well supported. Not surprisingly for Scotland's foremost school, piping and drumming are offered extramurally and bands have been known to tour the USA and Far East as well as performing closer to home. Kilts are worn by pupils on formal occasions such as Founder's Day or Open Days as well as for visits into Edinburgh for concerts etc. Fettes tartan kilts are worn by those who do not have their own family tartan.

In summary a traditional public school which seems to turn out well-rounded and confident young people. The striking school buildings are inspirational and of course, situated in Scotland's attractive capital Edinburgh means that pupils can benefit from many of the delights available in this cultural city. The vast open spaces of rural Scotland are within easy reach and provide endless opportunities for climbing, canoeing, fishing, golf, shooting etc. for hardy and adventurous souls. Academic results are pleasing and Fettes is run very much along the lines of a full boarding school. There is a good mix of girls and boys as well as a fair number of ex-pats and overseas students to create a healthy balance. If you fancy a change from the south east public school environment, do fly out to Edinburgh and visit this renowned school which in my view has a great deal to offer. After all it did not do too bad a job of Tony Blair and James Bond possessed all the essential qualities of the archetypal English, or should I say, British gentleman!

GLENALMOND COLLEGE

Perth

Perth and Kinross PH1 3RY

www.glenalmondcollege.co.uk

01738 842056

A SCOTTISH public school with an English accent! Admittedly, old boy Robbie Coltrane (Hagrid in the Harry Potter story) has a slight Scottish lilt, but I have personally never meet a single chap educated at this school who sounded anything other than an upper middle class Englishman from Hampshire. Perhaps this is to be expected from a school whose motto Floreat Glenalmond (Let Glenalmond Flourish) is similar to the Eton motto of Floreat Etona. However, there is still some debate as to whether Fettes or Glenalmond is the true Eton of Scotland and interestingly, Prince Charles, the heir to the throne was educated at the other well known Scottish public school Gordonstoun !

The school was founded in 1847 by W E Gladstone who was keen that it should be located north of the Firth and well away from any large town. The impressive school buildings are situated on the River Almond, a tributary of the mighty Tay and a notable salmon river in its own right. Glenalmond has always been reasonably popular with landed Highland families and other old money types who opted to stay local rather than head south to Eton, Harrow or Rugby. Naturally, the school still retains a degree of fascination for the Lairds and their friends, but not surprisingly, an increasing number of pupils from south of the border have also discovered that strolling around the school on Sundays wearing a kilt can be rather fun! English parents seeking a full boarding school for their sons or daughters have come to realise that this place is very much like a traditional English public school but with a Scottish flavour. The fact that they prepare students for A- levels rather than Scottish Highers helps to reinforce this image. Moreover, the school is miles away from the industrial belt, and the nearby city of Perth, some 8 miles away, is one of the few remaining parts of Scotland where the Conservative party still retains a notable presence.

Glenalmond is a relatively small co-educational school with approximately 400 pupils. The vast majority are full boarders and the pupils are allocated into one of eight boarding Houses, five for boys and three for girls. Boarding fees at £27,162 per annum are some three thousand pounds cheaper than English schools such as Eton, Marlborough or Charterhouse, but still staggeringly high. Until 1990 Glenalmond was an all boys' school, but it is now co-educational throughout and out of the 400 pupils about 40% are girls. Some 15% of the pupils come from overseas and the school presently has boys and girls from China, Russia, Germany, France, Spain, Mexico, Hong Kong and Scandinavia. This is a proper seven days a week boarding school and there is no sloping off on Saturday afternoons. In fact if you wish, you can board throughout the term without having to leave at weekends. Glenalmond is unquestionably the ideal school for the outdoor types and the majority of pupils who chose to come here would consider themselves a hardy bunch. Some of the many activities on offer include fishing, canoeing, climbing, kayaking, rock climbing, golf, polo and skiing.

Admission to Glenalmond starts from the age of 12 years, right up to Sixth Form. Children come from schools across Scotland and the rest of the United Kingdom. It is not unusual for boys to come from prep schools in the south east of England such as Cothill House, Oxfordshire, or Cottesmore in West Sussex. Prep schools in East Anglia also send a few boys to Glenalmond as do northern schools such as Aysgarth in

North Yorkshire. Understandably, local schools in Perthshire are well represented and many join the school from overseas. Entry to the school at 13+ is via the Common Entrance Examination set externally but marked at Glenalmond, or the Academic Scholarship examination set and marked by the school. Sixth Form entry requires a minimum of five GSCEs at grade B or above. Glenalmond , is not generally thought of as a top league academic institution, but then again it is hardly a school for slackers. Academic results are on the whole reasonably good and whilst better than Gordonstoun, and on par with Loretto, they are definitely less impressive than Fettes. Last year a satisfactory 5% won places at Oxford or Cambridge. The vast majority of leavers progress to some sort of higher educational institution with a good number ending up at prestigious Russell Group universities.

By now you have probably clicked that this school is big on sport and outdoor pursuits. Certainly, sporting activities form an integral part of life at Glenalmond , and facilities are excellent. Over the years the school has won many trophies, with a number of O.Gs attaining national and international honours. The school is justly proud of its long tradition of sporting excellence. Glenalmond has a strong rugby tradition and the 1st XV play on Neish's which sits on raised ground above the junior pitches. Notable rugby players who have been educated at Glenalmond include former Scotland and Lions Rob Wainwright and David Sole, as well as current Scotland international Dougie Hall.

The following account of life at Glenalmond has been written by my good friend Dr Keith Thomson who has a close association with the school:

Dr Keith D Thomson (1961-65)

The school was founded in 1847 by W E Gladstone and still has a strong Episcopal tradition with the beautiful chapel at the centre of college life, it being important that all 400 pupils and the teaching staff are able to attend chapel services at the same time. A magnificent brand new Harrison organ was installed in 2007. In December 2006 I was proud to attend the London OG (Old Glenalmond) dinner at the Caledonian Club in Halkin Street with my daughter Rebecca (1996-2000) and son Duncan (1997-2002) – perhaps a unique first in the history of the school since girls have only been included since 1990. I will never forget Thursday 29th August 1996 when on a social visit to show my daughter her dad's old school, the Warden (Headmaster) said to her, "What are you doing next Tuesday, how about coming here?" She thought for a second and said, "Yes as long as my horse can come too." Which it did!

A year later after viewing several English schools within two hours drive of our home in Ascot, including St Edward's Oxford, Bradfield, Pangbourne and Charterhouse we took Duncan up to Glenalmond. It was a miserable, wet typically "driech" Scottish day with a low mist covering the usually spectacular backdrop of the Scottish Highlands. The bedroom facilities on offer in my old house (Skrines) were of the "loosebox" variety. Two current staff members had also taught me 30 years before! I remember saying to him after the visit, "Was there anything you liked about the school?" His immediate reply was, "Yes Dad, everything." My daughter not only scored the first lacrosse goal for the school team but in 1999 captained the school to their first ever victory at the Scottish Schools Equestrian Championship at Gleneagles. In her final year she was head girl and head of the CCF. Duncan became a house prefect, head of the CCF and was a member of successful basketball and tennis teams. I enjoyed my four years at Glenalmond (1961-65) in spite of compulsory early morning cold baths during the summer term (these were not obligatory at Gordonstoun). There was beautiful scenery, salmon fishing in the river and a strong sporting and competitive ethos. Certainly the geographical features were not part of the scene in Edinburgh schools like Fettes which I guess might boast of the ex-PM as its most famous former pupil. Sadly to say in this day and age a major advantage must be that drug dealers are less likely to be at the school gates when it is so far from the nearest town. I was in the shooting eight which was well placed in the Ashburton Shield at Bisley in 1964 and 1965. I envy my children being there when it was a "mixed" boarding school, as a result they are both relaxed and confident with members of the opposite sex. One criticism from my day was the obsession with pupils gaining entry, preferably with a scholarship, to Oxbridge. Other universities (e.g. Edinburgh, where I went) did not have such status. I hope this attitude has now changed. I have been to many London OG dinners and always meet interesting and well balanced men of all ages with whom I often find an instant bond – the "old school tie" seems to be still very much alive and kicking. The guest speakers are always former pupils who are known public *persona*, for example Sandy Gall (BBC News), former CBI President Adair Turner, Chancellor Lord Falconer and in 2006, Major Phil Ashby who gave a graphic account of his escape from machete-wielding RUF rebels in Sierra Leone in 2000.

I am delighted with the social prowess, academic attainments, strong work ethic and general zest for life that both my own OG children possess and have no hesitation in recommending Glenalmond College to other parents, even those who live south of the border, as the school is situated in beautiful countryside 10 miles from Perth and only 45 minutes drive from Edinburgh Airport.

GORDONSTOUN

Elgin

Moray IV30 5RF

www.gordonstoun.org.uk

01343 837829

FOUNDED by a German refugee, Dr Kurt Hahn, the school attended by Prince Charles is a relative newcomer having been established in 1933, several centuries after Eton the Alma Mater of his two sons, the Duke of Cambridge and Prince Harry. Other members of the British Royal Family have also been alumni here including Princes Anne and her children. Apparently, Dr Hahn had turned down the offer to take up the position of Headmaster at Eton in order to establish Gordonstoun. This educational establishment may be "new" but, the school does boast two very striking old buildings dating back to the 17th century and of course, many later additions to the 150 acres site. Gordonstoun is located in the outstandingly beautiful and sparsely populated area of north east Scotland known as Moray, a part of the country blessed with excellent salmon rivers and great distilleries of fine malts. It is a corner of Britain where I have spent many happy weeks in pursuit of the king of fish!

Like all good public schools Gordonstoun offers a well balanced and rounded education. However, it is important to realise that whilst the school's main priority is to allow the pupils to achieve their full potential, it is not renowned as an overly academic institution and places little importance on league tables. Examination results are satisfactory and approximately half of the pupils achieve A and B grades at A-level. However, the vast majority of boys and girls do go on to university, and a few win places at Oxford and Cambridge. That said, parents looking at this school should look beyond exam results and consider the importance of Gordonstoun's Four Pillars: Challenge, Service, Internationalism and Responsibility. The school prides itself on preparing students through learning by diverse experiences and become international citizen in a rapidly changing world. Surely these are qualities of immense importance which most of us would like our children to leave school with. For more details on the Four Pillars, please check the school's website

Admission to Gordonstoun is not too competitive and the assessment consists of an interview, a reference from the candidate present school and an examination. Entry at 13+ is via the Common Entrance Examination, scholarship or a special exam for those not attending a prep school. The so called Gordonstoun's Family consists of one third of pupils from Scotland, one third from the rest of the U.K. and one third from a large number of overseas countries. This healthy balance most certainly leads to an interesting and diverse community. Entry into the Sixth Form requires a minimum of five GCSEs at grade C or better.

Gordonstoun is a progressive co-educational boarding school for approximately 600 boys and girls. About 500 are full boarders and the remaining 100 day pupils. There are in total nine boarding Houses, six for boys and three for girls. Two of the Houses, Altyre and Gordonstoun are Sixth Form boys Houses. Gordonstoun House generally referred to as G-House is home to 24 boys and it is situated on the top floor of the central 17th century mansion. Popular features of House life include: inter-house competition, expeditions and in-house evenings. The students are supported by the Housemaster/mistress, assistant Housemaster/mistress, Matron and Tutors. They are all there to help and ensure that the pupils do not stray from the straight and narrow. Thankfully, there are no big cities nearby to distract from the many outdoor activities such as sailing, climbing etc. which this school is justly famous for. Seamanship has been part of the curriculum since the school began and Gordonstoun has its own yacht: The Ocean Spirit of Moray.

The pastoral care at the school is really first rate and parents who are anxious about Gordonstoun past reputation as a harsh institution need not worry. The school's ethos still places a high emphasis on discipline and physical education, especially outdoor activities such as mountaineering and seamanship, but cold showers and punishment runs are now a thing of the past. Moreover, with 100 teachers at the school there are plenty of experienced adults around to keep an eye on things and the student-teacher ratio is one of the lowest in the country. This is all well and good and highly commendable. However, one needs to appreciate that Gordonstoun is somewhat different and many view it as an alternative option in the public school world.

The school is terribly outdoorsy with sailing, seamanship and expeditions being compulsory for all students. All other major sports such as rugby, football, cricket, hockey, golf, tennis, swimming and shooting are all excellently catered for. The rugby team has in recent years toured Argentina, Chile and South Africa. The Duke of Edinburgh Awards were initiated at Gordonstoun and this activity is still strongly promoted at the school. Community service is paid more than just lip service here and all students become members of one of the public service ranging from Coastguard to Fire Service.

To summarise, this is a public school with an alternative slant. Not terribly academic but strong on character building and pastoral care. Discipline is still emphasised and some feel that the school is run with military precision. Extremely strong on the outdoor activities and great emphasis is placed on civic duties. The school has close ties with Germany and educates a large number of overseas pupils. Student exchanges with schools abroad help to forge international links which in our global economy can be vitally important. As for its social standing, had Prince William and Prince Harry followed in their father and grandfather's footsteps and come to study at Gordonstoun, the school would still be highly fashionable with the English Sloaney set. As it happens, for reasons which I am not privy to, they went to Eton and the rest is history.

GRESHAM'S SCHOOL

Holt

Norfolk NR25 6EA

www.greshams.com

01263 714500

DRIVING up to Gresham's School through East Anglia into North Norfolk you'd be forgiven for thinking that you were on the road to nowhere. However, drive on for a while longer and you will soon come across the beautiful market town of Holt where Gresham school is to be found. Located just a few miles from the fashionable North Norfolk coastline this affluent and tranquil town seems caught in a golden time warp, reminiscent of an era which many of us in the south east have long forgotten.

This co-educational, day and boarding school was established in 1555 and originally operated from Sir John Gresham's manor house in Holt. By 1859 the school had been rebuilt and soon after acquired an additional 200 acres of land which now offer a very wide variety of playing fields and sports facilities. 30 tennis courts, a double AstroTurf, six rugby pitches, football, netball, athletics track and cross country course are just a few of the outdoor opportunities available. Two indoor sports halls cater for dance, trampolining, basketball and badminton amongst a host of other activities.

The school has its own prep and pre-prep schools and many of those children progress naturally into the senior school. Admission is via the Common Entrance examination and you would need to register 18 months before entry. However, if your current school does not prepare for Common Entrance then the schools own exam in Maths and English would be written. There are a number of scholarships on offer covering academic, music, art, sport or drama and all will grant 15% remission of fees. The Gresham's Foundation which was established in 2006 is also able to offer means tested bursaries to pupils who would otherwise be unable to afford a Gresham's education. The school has worked very hard on fundraising for large capital projects, the last major one being the building of the Auden Theatre. Drama is compulsory for all students until GCSE level, thereafter however, an enormous number still participate in the school productions which are put on several times a year. The theatre is professionally run and fully equipped. This gives pupils the opportunity not only to act but to learn about the technical side of stage management and theatre production. In addition the Nicholson Gallery hosts exhibitions and courses, all of which are widely used and appreciated by the local community as well as the school.

Academically, Gresham's is sound but most definitely not an examination factory. Placed 346 in the Financial Times Independent Schools Table, it is lags well behind some of its potential competitors such as Uppingham 193rd, Rugby 172nd and Oundle at an incredible 40th. However these competitors are much larger schools and we are firm believers in using league tables merely as a guide. In 2011 30.4% of A-Levels were graded A* A. Gresham's still manages to secure 7% of their pupils a place at Oxford or Cambridge and 98% of students go on to University. Particularly bright children take part in the gifted and talented programme which includes the "Colloquium" a club to encourage critical thinking and debate. Looking at the list of old boys and girls there seems to be quite a nod to politics and public service as well as a large number of pupils who achieve highly in the arts. Greshams most famous old boy would have to be Benjamin Britten, a composer whose name is synonymous with the very best of British Opera. 2013 marks the 100th anniversary of Britten's birth and Gresham's has planned an entire year of events to showcase his works.

There are only about 500 pupils at Gresham's Senior just over half of whom are boarders. The seven very individual Houses each accommodate approximately 70 children, both full boarders and day pupils are part of each House. There is a resident Housemistress or Housemaster for each house, supported by a Matron and a number of tutors. There is a very strong sense of community within the Houses and children are really encouraged to play a full role in Gresham life. The appointed tutor will be responsible for your child throughout the senior years and the relationship that is formed is highly beneficial. The majority of pupils come from families based in East Anglia and Norfolk but there is also a fairly large contingent of overseas students. Currently numbering around 75 these boys and girls, who come from as close as Switzerland and Germany, to as far away as Japan and China, all seem to integrate extremely well into the school. The lasting impression of Gresham's is a word which we have used repeatedly throughout the profile of this school: community. It is in the way the school is a part of the local environs. It is at the heart of how the school is run and it is most definitely visible in the way the children are enveloped by the care and support of the staff and fellow pupils.

Mario di Monaco and Kerry Rhodes

HAILEYBURY

Haileybury

Hertford SG13 7NU

www.haileybury.herts.sch.uk

01992 463353

THE striking building in which the school still stands was built in 1806 as a training college for employees of the East India Company. Haileybury, was actually founded in 1862, and occupies 500 acres of countryside in Hertfordshire, near the town of Hertford. The school is now a wonderful blend of old and new buildings with the "Quad" reputed to be the largest academic quadrangle in Britain and one of the largest in the world. It is conveniently located some 20 miles north of London and approximately 30 miles south of Cambridge. Heathrow, Luton and Stansted airports as well as the M25 are all a short distance away. For decades this renowned educational establishment enjoyed a reputation as a national school for the sons of families who ran the British Empire. However, the complexion of the school has somewhat changed and Haileybury is now less grand than it used to be probably because, as it has been the case with many other public schools, the domestic catchment area has shrunk to a radius of about 40 miles. Nowadays, boys and girls tend to come primarily from North London and the counties of Hertfordshire, Essex, Bedfordshire, Cambridgeshire and Buckinghamshire. A fair number hail from abroad.

In common with many of the public schools founded during the same period, Haileybury, was for many years, a traditional all-boys boarding school with a reputation for being good at churning out young men destined for the Army or the Colonies. Apparently, only Eton and

119

Harrow can claim more Victoria Crosses than Haileybury. However, nothing in life remains the same indefinitely and like many other public schools it has had to embrace co-education and day places in order to reflect contemporary parental requirements. Girls now make up 40% of the intake and out of a total of 750 pupils a respectable 63% are boarders. The sizeable day contingent however, does not imply that this school is losing its boarding pedigree. The vast majority of the day pupils are current or former members of the Haileybury Lower School (11+ entry) which as one would expect appeals to local parents. Day places for the main school at 13+ or sixth form entry are limited and the few that are accepted by the boarding Houses are welcomed on the understanding that they accept and support the school's boarding ethos.

The senior school has 12 boarding Houses each accommodating approximately 55 pupils. Contrary to what many parents believe, there is no flexi or weekly boarding at Haileybury and the school most definitely remains operational throughout the weekends. Having said that, the school's prospectus states that "there is no pressure on boarders to remain after Saturday afternoon commitments are over nor is there any expectation that they should depart". Of course if your parents live in Russia or China departing for 24 hours is not a viable option. However, most of the alumni from Herts, Bucks, Beds etc. do tend to go home most weekends and return on Sunday evening in time for chapel service. Admittedly, this set up may not appeal to everyone but, an increasing number of families seem to like the idea of having their offspring home most weekends and I have personally known parents who have opted for Haileybury for this very reason. However, one must not imagine for one minute that this works out any cheaper. The main school fees at Haileybury are £ 27,384 for boarders and £ 20,565 for day places. In other words just as expensive as Stowe, Radley or Rugby.

On a slightly frivolous note I would like to digress into the amusing but nevertheless important area of social class and private education. The original Sloane Ranger Handbook published in 1982, listed this school as a Sloane choice but grouped it with the second XI. However, the revised book by Peter York and Olivia Stuart-Liberty, which came out in 2008, seems to have dropped Haileybury as well as a number of other famous schools such as Oundle, Uppingham, Clifton, Bradfield and even Tony Blair's alma mater Fettes , from the Sloane list. Prince Charles old school Gordonstoun, also seems to have been sidelined! Why this should be the case is not clear as I am certain that most of these schools are still Sloaney to a degree. Maybe geography has something to do with it. Some schools are just too far from London whilst others may be located in "unfashionable" counties or are seen as too parochial. Moreover, "old money" has yet to recover from the Lloyd's debacle or the shock of being marginalised by the Americanisation of the City when the financial sector was deregulated in 1986.Many traditional public school families simply can no longer afford the spiralling costs of a boarding school education. On the other hand, many of the newly rich who live in London or the Home Counties seem to have no problems in finding the cash for the eye-watering fees. These so called "first time buyers" have now become fairly prevalent at major public schools like Haileybury and together with the increasing band of pupils from abroad, are keeping many private schools in fine fettle.

Modern day Haileybury is a dynamic and successful co-educational school offering a progressive education in a caring, friendly and traditional environment. Entry into the school is competitive but not excessively so. Haileybury is not renowned as an academic hot house but parents who are focussed on examination results or Oxbridge places should not overlook this school as they certainly have the ability to cater for the very brightest as well as the average candidate. There are three entry points at 11+, 13+ and 16+. Pupils who join at 11 enter the Lower School provided they have performed to an acceptable level in the entrance tests in maths, English, verbal and non verbal reasoning. At 13+ the Common Entrance Examination at the candidate's own prep school is used and Haileybury require a 55% pass mark for boarders and 65% for day places. Academic, music and sport scholarships are available but, don't expect them to lighten the financial burden considerably as they are only worth a maximum of 10% of the fees. Sixth form entry is limited to a hand full of places. Apparently, girls attending single sex day schools but wishing to switch to a co-ed school with boarding facilities are keen to snap up these coveted places before embarking on a university degree. A friend's daughter did exactly this and then went on to study medicine at Southampton University.

Examination results at Haileybury are consistently good for a moderately selective school with a diverse intake. Students can study for the traditional "A" levels or take the I.B. which is popular and well established at Haileybury. The A*A/B pass rate for "A" levels was a commendable 85% in 2011 and the Oxbridge/U.C.L. success rate a respectable 8%. Comparison with rival schools is always interesting and in 2011 the highly regarded Financial Times academic league tables for senior private schools, placed Haileybury in the 199th position. The school fared less well than Radley 23rd, Harrow 39th, Oundle 40th and Rugby 172nd. However, Haileybury did score higher than Wellington 220th, Bedford School 256th, St. Edwards 483rd, Stowe 529th and Felsted 594th.

On the sport front, the facilities are exceptional with acres of playing fields and one of only 13 rackets-courts in the country. The swimming pool complex is particularly impressive having won national awards for its design. There are 12 tennis courts and glass-backed squash courts. The main sports for boys are rugby, cricket, football, hockey, swimming and tennis and for girls hockey, lacrosse, netball, tennis and swimming. Needless to say, with all those acres to utilise, games are taken very seriously at this school and professional coaches are not unheard of. Rugby is still played passionately, however, with girls making up 40% of the school's intake there are less rugby players to choose from than was the case when the school was all boys. It is fair to say that Haileybury is no longer the rugby force it once was. Football on the other hand has become popular and played to a competitive level with notable successes.

No article about Haileybury is complete without mentioning some of the famous alumni who have been educated at this renowned school. On the military front, 17 Old Haileburians have been awarded the Victoria Cross. Eton and Harrow with 36 and 19 V.C.s respectively may occupy the top two spots, but nevertheless Haileybury's success in this field is still quite exceptional bearing in mind that Eton of course, is a much larger school. In fact for a school which is not particularly big, Haileybury has a surprisingly long list of famous people who have excelled in very diverse fields. Well known Old Boys include: Clement Attlee - former Prime Minister, Rudyard Kipling - author, Sir Stirling Moss - racing driver, Alan Ayckbourn – dramatist and Lord Sainsbury - businessman.

The all boys boarding and day prep school which our two sons attend, usually sends one or two boys per year to Haileybury. Over time we have become acquainted with a fair number of Haileybury families and the vast majority have spoken very positively about the school. Most feel that it is a rounded and academically sound place with excellent extracurricular activities to satisfy all types. Naturally, having spent five years at a traditional boarding school, most of the students possess the charm and confidence associated with elite public schools. Most of the Haileyburian who I have met over the years have been gentlemen to the core without any traces of arrogance or pompousness.

HARROW SCHOOL

Harrow on the Hill

Middlesex HA1 3HP

www.harrowschool.org.uk

0208 872 8007

AS the alma mater of 7 British Prime Ministers including Winston Churchill, numerous royals and countless aristocrats, Harrow can justifiably claim to be the second best know school in the English speaking world. Founded in 1572 with the blessing of Elizabeth 1st, the school which accommodates just over 800 boys sits on top of a hill in North West London occupying 350 acres. Its delightful red brick buildings are part of a quaint village that looks and feels a world apart from the surrounding uninspiring suburbia immortalised by the poet Sir John Betjeman. Sir John, who was educated at Marlborough, may have had issues with the sprawling rows of post war semis encroaching upon the school's perimeter but, he held Harrow in high esteem and judging by his many complementary remarks, I suspect that he was rather fond of this school.

Harrow has had more than its fair share of ups and downs over the years and on occasions has had to dig deep to stay afloat. However, that is all in the long and distant past and modern day Harrow is a cutting edge and highly successful school achieving phenomenally good results. When the ambitious Barnaby Lenon took over as Headmaster in 1999, Harrow stepped into a higher gear and the school zoomed into the academic premier league. By the time he left in 2011 Harrow was achieving A-level results way above the private schools average. In 2010 the A*/A levels pass rate came in at an impressive 75% which was better than Radley, Wellington or Marlborough but not as good as Winchester or Eton. Moreover, 18% of boys gain places at Oxbridge most years with Oxford being considerably more popular than Cambridge. Other favoured destinations include Bristol, Durham, Edinburgh, Newcastle, U.C.L. and Imperial. American Ivy League colleges such as Yale, Harvard, Princeton and Brown have also become desirable for those who can afford them. Neither the I.B. nor the Pre-U have been introduced at Harrow and the school like Eton and Radley only offers A-levels.

Old customs continue in a timeless fashion at this school and Harrow remains a single sex full boarding school where boys wear traditional uniforms (one for week days and one for Sundays) including the famous straw hat. Sunday best consists of black tails, pinstriped trousers, waist coats and black tie. Add a top hat and fancy cane for prefects who are known as monitors. Also, there are no immediate plans to admit girls or day pupils and the Headmaster was at pain to stress that full boarding at Harrow means no sloping off on Saturday afternoons to spend the rest of the weekend away from school. Sundays are packed with structured activities and as tradition dictates boys are required not set foot off the hill.

Although the school's geography is not to every ones liking, there seems to be no shortage of applicants to Harrow. This school is massively oversubscribed as well as increasingly difficult to get in. There is a general consensus amongst current parents that the entry bar has been quietly raised over the last ten years and consequently securing a place has become more competitive. Having said that, selected candidates are only required to obtain an average of 60% in Common Entrance which is less onerous than what is expected at Eton, Winchester or Westminster. However, Barnaby Lennon did say that the majority of boys offered places at Harrow obtain over 70% in the Common Entrance exam. Also, contrary to common belief there is absolutely no need to register your son with the school soon after birth as it was once the norm. Harrow accepts applications any time from birth right up to the age 10 and there are no great advantages in registering early. The school has its own entry assessment (see Harrow web site for details) which takes place when the boys are 11. Conditional offers are made to those who perform well and some boys may be placed on a waiting list. A number of places are left open for late developers who are keen to come to Harrow or good candidates who may have applied late.

In 2010 Harrow featured in a channel four television documentary entitled "Too poor for posh school". The cameras followed the fortunes of a group of bright 11 year old boys from low income homes who were attending state schools, competing amongst themselves for a Beckwith scholarship. Thanks to the generosity of Old Harrovian Sir Peter Beckwith, the school offers two places per year with up to 100% of the fees paid, for boys aged 11 to attend two years at a prep school before coming to Harrow aged 13. Rather surprisingly for a programme of this nature, over two million people tuned in to watch it and predictably it provoked a fairly lively debate. Some people wondered if it was morally correct to pluck underprivileged boys from their normal social environment and thrust them into an elite public school. Others felt that Harrow deserved great credit for giving these "rough diamonds" a polished education virtually free, which under normal circumstances would have cost an eye watering £ 30,000 per annum.

In a country which remains preoccupied with class one should not be surprised to discover that many parents view the social standing of a particular public school with more than just a passing interest. In this respect Harrow, like its rival Eton, has always had a reputation for attracting the higher classes and to a lesser degree this is still the case. However, we have come a long way from 1923 when Old Harrovian

Prime Minister, Stanley Baldwin, packed his new Cabinet with six other Harrovians and announced that he wanted his Government to be one that Harrow would be proud of! Fast forward to 2012 and the school is represented in politics by only three M.P.s and none of them sit in the David Cameron's Cabinet. Nowadays, there is a more meritocratic feel to the school and 50% of the boys are the sons of successful middle class professionals from London and the Home Counties. The types who own large chunks of Norfolk or Northumberland are still around, but they are far less prevalent than they used to be. Moreover, families who may be inclined to dismiss this school as too exclusive should bear in mind that 20% of the boys at Harrow receive financial assistance from the school presumably because their parents are unable to afford the full fees.

The old rivalry that has existed for centuries between Eton and Harrow is now mainly confined to the sport fields. The annual cricket match involving these two schools, first held in 1805, is still played at Lords and although it is not the great social event it once was, it remains a keenly contested special occasion. For those interested in Royal sports, Windsor Park plays host to a yearly polo tournament sponsored by Jack Wills. This rather jolly day out, pitches Eton against Harrow, Oxford versus Cambridge and Harvard take on their American rival Yale. Eton it seems, no longer has it all its own way and in recent years Harrow has had some notable success over its rival in rugby as well as cricket and polo. Unlike Eton however, Harrow is not a major rowing school and therefore highly unlikely to qualify for the Princes Elizabeth cup at Henley let alone winning it! In general Harrow, remains a serious sporting school where success on the rugby or cricket pitches is still greatly celebrated.

Should your son lack the robust sporting skills required to make the top teams at this school do not despair. The performing arts are represented to a very high standard. The Ryan Theatre, a state of the art venue that seats almost 400 people, has an orchestra pit, full time wardrobe mistress and two full time technicians. Around 14 productions are put on each year. This facility could hold its own in the West End. Also as one would expect from the school that has given us the musician James Blunt, boys with musical talents are held in very high esteem. The vast majority of boys play an instrument and many play two or three.

At Harrow, perhaps more than any other public school, it pays to research the Houses carefully before deciding which one to choose. The boarding Houses have an ancient order and to some parents the tradition of a particular House seems to matter more than the reputation of the Housemaster. That said, things are changing and the school is now keen to ensure that each House has a balanced mixture of boys with different skills and from diverse backgrounds. Historically, Elmfield and the Grove used to be amusingly referred to as the "grouse moor" Houses as they used to be popular with the fishing and shooting set from the shires. By and large boys who end up in these Houses tend to come from boarding country preps such as Aysgarth in North Yorkshire. Other Houses such as Newlands used to be known as the London House, presumably because many of its boys came from the capital and not the country. There is also a brand new house called Lyon's which as one would expect, is relatively spacious and designed for the 21st century. The draw- back of course, as one conservative old army type told me, is that it lacks tradition. By the way whilst on the subject of the army let us not forget the strong historical link which this school has had with the Armed Forces. Incredibly for a medium sized school, an impressive 19 Old Harrovians have been awarded the Victoria Cross so far.

No article about this school can ever be complete without mentioning the Harrow Songs. These are sung by Old Harrovians throughout the world and the most famous is "Forty Years On". Winston Churchill was a great enthusiast for songs and during the Second World War he was often to be heard belting out "St Joels" from his bath! Churchill's Songs is a unique event held at the school every year and on very special occasions it takes place in the Royal Albert Hall. The history of Harrow Songs dates back to 1860 and one which I particularly enjoy is a solo entitled "Five Hundred Faces", which conveys the feelings of a young arrival at the school:

Five hundred faces, and all so strange!

Life in front of me, home behind,

I felt like a waif before the wind

Tossed on an ocean of shock and change.

P.S. In 2011 Harrow school appointed James Hawkins as Headmaster replacing the retiring Barnaby Lenon. We wish Mr Hawkins every success at the helm of this great school.

Reflections on Malvern College by Andrew Knott and Edward Davenhill

I have to confess a strong bias in writing this; I was brought up in the grounds of Malvern College from the age of one month, attended the school myself and watched my parents live out 33 wonderful years in the College community. But some might feel that this is ancient history and so I consulted my nephew, Edward Davenhill, the youngest of three brothers to attend the school, for his up to date reflections of his time there which finished in 2010. It is reassuring and not altogether surprising to discover that things that shaped and benefitted his time at Malvern were, by and large, the same as mine. It is not that things have remained unchanged in the school, it is always improving and developing, but in its DNA are the core beliefs that make the school a wonderful cradle for success and fulfilment in young people.

So what is not to like about Malvern College? Is it the magnificent backdrop of the Malvern Hills offsetting the beautiful Victorian sandstone school buildings and Chapel? Or in the other direction the equally spectacular views across the immaculate Senior cricket pitch to the Vale of Evesham. This school must surely have one of the most stunning venues of all the wonderful campus boarding schools in country.

From the point when the Victorians decided to replace the dwindling spa "industry" with schools, Malvern has been an academic centre of excellence. Whilst the numbers of independent schools around the town has consolidated, always at the forefront has been Malvern College. The merger with Ellerslie, one such girls' school, and Hillstone and The Downs prep schools some years ago resulted in the College becoming a superlative, full service educational provider in its own right.

Malvern College remains amidst the most exciting and forward-thinking phase of its existence. Demand for places is over capacity, more so than it has ever been, demonstrating that with its stunning location, facilities and broad achievements, the school draws pupils from around the country and the world. In the ever increasingly multi-cultural, global community in which we live, the integration of pupils from across such diverse backgrounds can only be a good thing and clearly demonstrates that an investment in first-class education at Malvern College remains the number one priority for many families.

However, schooling is not only about a stunning campus and beautiful views, it is about a whole of life experience with the academic endeavours clearly at the forefront. The focus of the school was and remains an ethos that strives to ensure that each pupil has the opportunity to find and develop the characteristics that for so many are the core of what will shape them and their lives. The belief and encouragement to try everything that the school has to offer ensures that few leave without a lifelong passion for some activity which was seeded there.

Academic pursuits should be and are at the centre of any school. For Malvern this has always meant striving to develop and improve how pupils are taught and learn. In the 1960's and 70's the school was the first independent school to have a foreign language laboratory and significantly helped to pioneer Nuffield method of teaching science – learning by doing experiments rather than just watching a teacher. This is now taken as the standard by most. In 1992 Malvern was one of the first public schools to introduce the option of studying the International Baccalaureate (IB) as an alternative to A Levels, providing the school with real knowledge and experience in the area and giving it a real edge over its rivals in terms of academic standing. The split is currently about 55/45 per cent in favour of the IB. The option to choose either of these courses in the Sixth Form attracts students with a greater academic ability from across this country and beyond. The resultant additional teaching qualifications achieved by the staff benefit the standards obtained by everyone across the board.

The engrained desire to always drive the school forward could have no better champions than current Chair of the Governors, Lord MacLaurin and the Headmaster, Antony Clark. Their energy and determination to improve, upgrade, augment and develop the school knows few bounds and clearly recognises the thesis that if the College is not moving forward, it will find itself falling behind.

In 2009, large scale development plans reached completion as two newly built, award winning, boarding houses officially opened. An existing boys' house moved into one, whilst a newly formed girls' house suitably called Ellerslie now inhabits the other. Whilst this hugely increases capacity, it also provides unparalleled living standards for a large proportion of the school. A longer-term refurbishment programme is ongoing amongst the remaining nine houses. Also opened in 2009 was the new sports complex, boasting an Olympic standard swimming pool, a state-of-the-art gym, a double sized sports hall, studio, shooting range, cricket centre and climbing wall, as well as entertainment and function rooms equipped with fully serviced catering. The fantastic standards are epitomized by these facilities becoming the winter and wet weather training centre for Worcestershire County Cricket Club, a tie that demonstrably benefits cricket more broadly throughout the school. A new partnership with Worcester Warriors, the rugby union Premiership club, has developed the standards of another sport in the school, not bad for a once traditional football school! These developments were accompanied by an overhaul of the two existing rackets courts – showing the important balance of major and minor sports.

Sport as a whole thrives at the College and this camaraderie and team spirit remains long after leaving school. Cricket has a rich heritage at the College, with the 1st XI playing on the prestigious and immaculately maintained Senior. The Old Malvernians beat the Old Etonians in the Cricketer Cup Final in 2011, the third such win since the turn of the century. An Old Malvernian was a founding member of the Halford Hewitt (the public schools old boys' golf competition) which they won in 2006. In football, the school 1st XI reached the final of the ISFA Mercian League in 2009 and 2010, missing out by one goal in 2011. The OMs have triumphed in 17 of the 28 finals of the Arthur Dunn Cup – old boys' football competition. "The Ledder" which is an eight mile run across Herefordshire countryside and a clamber over the Malvern hills from Ledbury back to the school is the epitome of any sporting pupil's career at the College and is a long standing part of Malvern folklore.

The arts run core to life in the school with music, drama, dance, art and photography all given particular attention down to the finest details. Plans are underway to refurbish the Rogers Theatre.

But what of the character of the school? How does all this excellence manifest itself in school life? Perhaps the most appealing and unique advantage of life at Malvern is eating in houses. As opposed to the more common system of anonymous, central catering, dining in house provides an intimate, welcoming and collegiate atmosphere, developing a sense of community and spirit unique to each and every house. This sense of family and community is present in all aspects of the school and is central to the pastoral care and pupil staff relations that runs so strongly through the community. There is a balance to be struck in schools between being too big and losing contact with the pupils and being too small and not being able to offer sufficient facilities and opportunities. Malvern manages to achieve the ideal middle ground with outstanding facilities countered by the intimacy of de-centralised eating.

Malvern has always looked to expand the boundaries and opportunities offered to its pupils. Whether exploring the Brecon Beacons from the school's farmhouse, Cwm Llwch, or canoeing the white-waters of the Severn, Wye and Usk, or joining expeditions to climb and explore in the Cairngorms, Iceland, the Alps or the Himalayas (as I was privileged enough to do). It is the shared belief that a school, whilst primarily a place of learning, is the coming together of many elements, opportunities and shared experiences that will ignite the passion and potential in young people. The emphasis on individual achievement has its counterpoint in the encouragement of teamwork, co-operation and service to others. The benefit of these activities is only possible because of the devoted staff who understood how to get the most out of a pupil, inside and outside of the classroom.

One of the advantages of my "insiders" view point was observing the inner workings of the school after I had left but whilst the day to day operations were still clear in my mind. My overriding recollection was the shear care, dedication and kindness exhibited by all the staff to the pupils. It is only with this unique perspective that one can see the late night emails, discussions and correspondence to find a solution to an individual's problem or concern that would otherwise just be left to be as it was. The relationship and interaction between staff and pupils is surely the most vital and critical element of a successful school and my observations of Malvern were then and are now of a school that has this balance right. Once they are established and part of the fabric of school life, teaching staff and housemasters and mistresses are carried along by this successful formula for running the school.

When I asked Edward what he felt was the greatest benefit he gained from his time at Malvern, it was not his achievements, of which there were many, but it was the attitude with which he was recognised for attempting them. I quote "Malvern allows many people to thrive and achieve a high level of self confidence from being successful, but without any of the arrogance or pompousness that seems to characterise other public schools" Edward perfectly encapsulated how Malvern was when I was a pupil and how it remained in his time there "Everyone feels like a big part of the community because of the of the intimacy of the school, the friendliness of the staff and the spirit of togetherness in each house".

The school's motto is *Sapiens Qui Prospicit* or "wise is the one who looks ahead" and it is my belief that generations of staff and governors have each abided by this adage and have looked to build for the future with result that Malvern currently finds itself looking ahead to a thriving, fulfilled and very positive future.

MARLBOROUGH COLLEGE

Marlborough

Wiltshire SN8 1PA

www.marlboroughcollege.org

01672 892200

FOUNDED in 1843 with the aim of educating the sons of clergymen, Marlborough has a reputation as one of the most forward-looking independent schools. It was one of the first of the traditional Public schools to allow girls into the Sixth Form in 1968 and by 1989, it had become fully co-educational. Moreover, the school was also one of the first to introduce rugby and football as part of the formal curriculum, and as far back as the 1920s, decades before the others, abolished the controversial practice of fagging. The Anglican faith remains an important part of school life at Marlborough and a strong association with the Church of England remains. However, nowadays the sons of clergy make up a far smaller percentage of the school's population and other denominations are welcomed.

Generally regarded as one of the country's leading Public schools, this first division educational establishment is located some 8 miles south of junction 15 of the M4. Slip of the motorway and after a short drive through rolling Wiltshire countryside you will arrive at the delightful market town of Marlborough (population 9000). As we discovered when we visited the school, the sheer beauty of this seemingly affluent rural community can evoke nostalgic memories of a forgotten England far removed from our crowded and cosmopolitan south east. The immaculately kept school campus on the edge of the small town is a combination of original red brick buildings of a charming nature, interspersed with some tasteful new additions such as the large dining hall. Central Court is the school's main hub with some of the attractive buildings dating back to the 18th century. Virtually all of the 885 pupils are full boarders and girls make up approximately 38% of the school's population.

Entry into Marlborough is competitive but not viciously difficult. An assessment takes place in January during year seven and it is important to realise that this is not a pre-assessment but the real thing. If your son or daughter successfully overcomes the assessment hurdles, he or she will be offered a place subject to a satisfactory pass in the Common Entrance Examination. However, hardly anyone who has been given a place is turned away after Common Entrance. The latter though important, is primarily used as a "rubber stamping" exercise. Naturally, the school expects candidates to be academically competent and possess other attributes which will serve them well at Marlborough. A good prep school report is highly desirable, and the rest of the assessment consists of two interviews with senior masters as well as a computer test designed by Durham University which aims to gauge innate ability. It is almost impossible to prepare for the computer test so parents are strongly advised not to waste their time and money. After the assessment candidates may be offered a firm place on the A-list or placed on the B-waiting list. Inevitably, a number will fail and be advised to look elsewhere. Marlborough is a fashionable and highly sought after school which attracts a high number of applicants. The Duchess of Cambridge and Princess Eugenie have raised the school's profile to stratospheric levels so do not be too disappointed if your child fails to make the cut!

As one would expect from a forward-looking school, in recent years Marlborough has made some significant changes to its academic programme and in addition to A levels it now offers the I.B. for those seeking a broader curriculum and also the academically demanding Cambridge Pre-U. The school has also introduced the optional EPQ (Extended Project Qualification) for Sixth Formers. This challenging 6000 word research project is worth half an A-level and is highly regarded by universities as a measure of a pupil's research capability. However, with so many different qualifications on offer, compiling meaningful league tables has become a complex task. For example, a school that increasingly uses the rigorous Pre-U qualification may rank lower in the league tables than it did when it only offered A-levels, but unsurprisingly have a higher Oxbridge hit rate. The Financial Times 2011 tables for A-level results, ranked Marlborough a commendable 76th placing it well above some of its co-educational boarding rivals. Also impressive was the 12% Oxford and Cambridge success rate. The school's policy is to discourage "soft" A-levels and concentrate on the harder subjects likely to win places at the prestigious Russell Group universities rather than inflate less academic institutions with poorly qualified students.

After eight years at the helm, the Head Master Nicholas Sampson is leaving in July 2012 and a new Head has been appointed to take charge. When Mr Sampson took over in 2004, Marlborough was overwhelmingly British and still seen by many as a Sloane haven lacking social as well as ethnic diversity. Sampson clearly felt that the school's image needed to reflect modern Britain and he systematically set in place a programme of change designed to appeal to a wider and more diverse audience. Rather commendably, he seems to have made good progress and an increasing number of pupils now come from the State sector as well as from abroad. The introduction of a new and more open selection process has certainly helped to bring in new blood and siblings no longer seem to receive the same degree of preferential treatment they once did. Needless to say these welcome changes have not been acceptable to all and I am aware that the views of some of the genteel occupants of old Rectories dotted around Wiltshire, Hampshire and Berkshire have been less than complimentary.

As stated earlier, Marlborough is a full boarding school and it is important that parents realise that this place does not empty after Saturday afternoon games. Pupils are expected to spend the non-exeats weekends at school and participate in many of the structured activities available. There are 14 boarding Houses which are divided into two categories. The in-College Houses are the oldest and mainly gathered around the Central Court. Historically they have no names and are generally referred to by an alphanumeric title such as B1, C1, C2 and C3. The out-College Houses are newer and located further from the central school buildings. Most of the out-College Houses are mixed whereas the in-College Houses are single sex. When we visited the school we were given a tour of C1 one of the oldest of the boarding Houses which used to be a Coaching Inn. This charming boys House is apparently very popular and highly sought after. My son and I were highly impressed with what we saw and thoroughly enjoyed meeting the likeable Housemaster.

Marlborough has a deservedly strong reputation for sport which continues to play a central role in the ethos of the school. As one would expect from a famous and fashionable school charging boarding fees of £30,300 per annum, sporting facilities are second to none. The major sports for boys are rugby, cricket and hockey, whilst girls enjoy hockey, tennis and netball. Rugby games against their rival Radley, are always a lively affair and greatly anticipated. There are of course many other sports available including polo, shooting, fencing, swimming, golf, athletics, fives, water polo and lots more. No one at Marlborough needs to sit on the side line. There is something for every child to get stuck in and find their niche. The school is fortunate enough to be able to employ the service of professional coaches, many of whom can proudly boast their own impressive sporting achievements at national level.

Art, music and drama are all excellently catered for and the available facilities are top drawer. This school does not cut corners so one should not be surprised that a great deal of attention is paid to staging plays, concerts, art exhibitions etc. The large Victorian Gothic chapel serves as the spiritual centre of the school and boasts superb stained glass windows as well as collection of Pre-Raphaelites paintings. The strong Anglican foundation continues to permeate throughout the school and although pupils from all faiths are welcome, they are expected to subscribe to the schools philosophy and ethos. Educating boys and girls who will eventually become leaders in their chosen fields remains an important objective and many Marlburians will eventually become doctors, lawyers, bankers, businessmen or academics. Fewer pupils from Marlborough tend to join the Armed Forces nowadays, but we must not forget the school's 13 Victoria Cross holders and the many brave soldiers who perished during the World Wars.

So what makes this school appealing? I asked some of the boys at Marlborough this question and the answers were most revealing. Many liked the fact that the school was full boarding and co-educational. Interestingly, a few had turned down offers from single sex full boarding schools such as Harrow or Radley so that they could study and socialise with girls. Also high on the priority list was the close proximity of the many shops, pubs and cafes scattered around the town main streets. Being able to access these places on foot was clearly an experience which many pupils seemed to relish. The architectural beauty of the school and its rural location were also important factors for some. One boy was impressed by the fact that the school overlooked Wiltshire fields on one side and town buildings on the other. "We get the best of both worlds" is how he put it. One or two were unashamedly frank and were happy to admit that they had been drawn to Marlborough because of its "Designer Label" status which it seems to enjoy within certain social circles. Of course there is much to admire about this school that young boys and girls do not always appreciate. Good academic results, great pastoral care, progressive and innovative, first class teaching and a refreshingly

140

"unstuffy" image are just a handful of other things which this great school deserves credit for. In the words of the outgoing Head Master, Marlburians have an understated strength and do not necessarily need the limelight to shine. They can make immense contributions to society without shouting about it.

Like a number of other famous British Public schools, Marlborough has decided to establish its first overseas campus and Marlborough College Malaysia will open in 2012. This represents a significant development for the college and it is hoped that student exchange schemes can be set up. There have also been preliminary discussions with people from the East Coat of the United States and if things progress, a Marlborough College for the American Preppies may one day become a reality.

MERCHANT TAYLORS SCHOOL

Moor Park

Northwood HA6 2HT

www.mtsn.org.uk

01923 824644

FOUNDED in 1561 as one of the original "Great Nine" public schools, as defined by the Public Schools Act of 1868, Merchant Taylors School has a long and very distinguished history. Celebrating 450 years in 2011 they relocated from London to Moor Park in Middlesex in 1933 and being just a short walk from a Metropolitan Line station the school draws many of its 850 pupils from North West London Hertfordshire and Buckinghamshire. The geographic location of the school mirrors the multi ethnic North West London but set in around 250 acres, 55 of which are devoted to sports fields, one can hardly believe that one is just 35 minutes from central London.

With its position in any league table consistently in the top 10 Merchant Taylors is indeed a very academic institution. Large numbers of boys progress from local prep schools such as Northwood Prep, The Beacon in Amersham, St John's Prep Pinner and St Martin's in Northwood. Most enter at the age of 11 and competition for a place is fierce. Candidates sit the schools own entrance examination a year before entry, followed by an interview and the offer of a place. As with many schools there are a number of scholarships available although these are more of an honorarium in terms of financial value. However means tested bursaries, some available with up to 100% remission of the fees, ensure that the brightest boys do have the opportunity of receiving a first class education regardless of family background. The house system places each boy with a tutor, with whom he will remain for the duration of his stay at Merchant Taylors – usually to 18. This continuity of care works extremely well, the tutor being the first point of call for both parents and their son. Although most boys enter at the age of 11 you could still apply at 13 and 16. Although very much a personal choice my own preference is to keep my son at prep school until 13 by which point most boys have matured and developed a sense of responsibility.

Outside of the classroom there is the usual array of extra-curricular clubs, activities and sporting pursuits. Although the school is non-denominational there are opportunities to discuss religion in a variety of forums and there is a large chapel should you wish to attend services. This, unlike most other schools, is not compulsory. Rugby, cricket and hockey are all very popular - as are water sports on the schools own lakes. Particularly impressive though are the facilities available for art and music. Studios and practice rooms are available throughout the day, after school and on Saturdays. As a prospective parent I thought that slightly longer school week really encouraged boys to enjoy a much more well- rounded experience and not simply be stuck in an academic hot house for 5 years.

A Level results are outstanding particularly when one considers that MTS do not offer what one would consider as "soft options". Overall the AB pass rate last year was 95.9%. Breaking some of those down shows 85 boys taking Mathematics – 65 obtained A*As. Further Mathematics saw 19 boys sit the examination – a staggering 18 scored A*As. History, Politics, the Sciences, Economics and languages all do equally well. In recent years an average of around 20% of the pupils are offered a place at Oxford or Cambridge. Although one can get the impression that this is a very academic school full of rather "geeky" boys I'd say that actually isn't at all true. The sporting facilities are superb and all boys are expected to participate in either the Cadets, undertake the Duke of Edinburgh Awards or the schools own Community Service programme. The most notable of these is the school's link to PHAB (Physically Handicapped and Able Bodied) in which groups of sixth-formers, alongside girls from the nearby St Helen's School, run week long holiday camps for 20 handicapped youngsters each year. The funds required to facilitate the camp (approx £10 000) is raised annually by all boys at the school. This scheme has been running for more than thirty years and is something the school should be immensely proud of. Taking a look at the long list of famous old boys proves how well rounded the leavers are. From clergymen to Lancelot Andrewes, Bishop of Winchester, who translated and wrote the King James version of the Bible, the celebrated author Conn Iggulden, the hilarious Michael McIntyre, to a raft of professional sportsmen, politicians and poets

You may ask why Merchant Taylors has been included in this book, which is largely dedicated to boarding schools. Well it was simply the kind of school which could not be left out. Although the little boarding that they had has now gone entirely it is still run with the same very strong house ethos of a traditional boarding school. This is again reflected in the very smart uniform, dark suit, white shirt and the very proudly worn house tie. Add to that its reputation as the "St Pauls of North London". It is clear that the popularity of Merchant Taylors is set to increase as more middle class families who would have considered boarding are now financially squeezed into day schools which at around £15000 per annum are half of the £30000+ that you would expect to pay at Eton, Tonbridge, Winchester and the likes.

On visiting the school during their open day in May my lasting impressions were the sheer size and scale of both the buildings and grounds but most particularly the energy and enthusiasm of the teaching staff. It is clearly their aim to support and challenge every boy into completely fulfilling his potential.

MILLFIELD SCHOOL

Street

Somerset BA16 0YD

www.millfield.somerset.sch.uk

01458 442291

THERE may be a lot of readers who ask why Millfield has been included in this book. It doesn't meet the general definition of a traditional public school nor does it have an ancient history. Equally had we not included Millfield readers would have asked why not? The reputation of outstanding success is quite unprecedented in such a "new" school.

Established in 1935 by the educator and cricketer Rollo "Jack" Meyer, the philosophy at Millfield has remained one where the aim is to help every child develop their full potential. Meyer continued as Headmaster for 35 years. Unconventional, inclusive- regardless of sex, class, status or financial position Millfield broke the mould. Co-educational since 1939 the Millfield type, if it can possibly be called that, is simply a child who is ready to learn, shows enthusiasm and gets on with it. Whilst Millfield Prep School is a natural launching pad into the senior school, the school is popular not only countrywide but also has an overseas contingent of around 200 children representing 50 nationalities. An in house travel office assists pupils with all necessary arrangements.

You will need to register 18 months before the year of entry. Once registered your child's current school will be contacted for a confidential report. You will then be invited for an interview with a senior master as well as the Headmaster. After this assessment places are usually offered within a week. It is unusual for a school of this nature not to conduct an entrance exam (with the exception of those applying for scholarships) although Common Entrance results are used for setting purposes. Despite the school not being selective academically results are reasonably good at A-Level, in 2011 32% of pupils achieved A*/A grades and around 8% of pupils were offered places at Oxford and Cambridge. In all 95% go on to good universities. The ratio of staff to pupils is an incredible 1:6.5 and there are on average 12 pupils per class.

Approximately 900 of the 1200 pupils board. There are 19 houses, three of which are called country houses due to their location off of the main campus. Slightly less formal terminology than most public schools each House is managed by House parents and assistant house parents, 50-60 children reside in each house. Day pupils are split into four and are joined with boarders for activities and competitions and this ensures that day pupils are fully integrated into Millfield life. The chapel conducts a non-denominational service. All faiths are supported through the practicalities of getting to the church you would like to worship in, guidance on confirmations or discussions on anything at all with the chaplain.

Music, drama, theatre and the arts are all supported with absolutely first class teaching and facilities. Numerous theatres that seat hundreds equipped with state of the art gadgetry but more importantly than that talented pupils exhibiting skill and insight into their subjects far beyond what one would expect at senior school level.

However all these accolades pale in comparison to the successes Millfield enjoys in the sporting arena. In some ways it feels as if the school is a self contained sports academy. There is simply nothing at which it does not excel. The facilities are of Olympic competition standard and indeed so are many of the pupils both past and present. There are 130 staff sports coaches, the school prides itself on the policy that no child will be denied the opportunity to participate due to lack of ability, so no matter what level your child is pitching at there will be fantastic facilities and superb coaching to develop their potential to the highest level. With two golf courses, an indoor riding school, fencing salle, indoor tennis centre as well as outdoor courts, polo field, judo dojo and cricket pitches just to illustrate a few options any sport your son or daughter would like to take is covered at Millfield. 54 Olympians have attended this school and so it is most fitting that it has recently been confirmed that the Russian Swimming team will be using Millfield and its 50m pool as its training base for the London 2012 Olympic Games. So a perfect example of how easy it is to see where your fees of £10400 per term for boarders and just over £7000 per term for day pupils are being spent. On truly outstanding facilities and the very best of teaching that money can buy. Scholarships are available in all areas and range from 15% to 50% and in cases of real financial need means tested bursaries may be applied for.

Famous Old Millfieldians are found in all walks of life. Tony Blackburn – radio broadcaster, Stewart Copeland – musician, Lily Allen – singer, Jason Connery – actor, Sophie Dahl – model/author, John Sargeant – BBC political journalist and surprising hero of Strictly Come Dancing! A host of international sporting heroes; Gareth Edwards, Matt Perry, Olly Morgan, Will Matthews, Robin Lett, Simon Jones, Mark Foster and Anthony Allen – a few names that barely scratch the surface. However as with all schools, this one will not suit every child, Millfield is probably not best for a quiet retiring type and its modern, liberal, highly competitive focus engenders a love it or hate it reaction. In spite of being quite a traditionalist I loved it and would definitely recommend that you consider it for your shortlist.

Robert Marshall, Millfield Pupil, 1982-1987

"Really good at sport" is on most occasions the reaction of people when you mention that you went to school there. I have always felt this is deeply unfair to a school that has so much more to offer, its facilities are un-rivalled and while its sporting achievements will always stand out and be the first port of call to many aspiring sportsman, if you have a passion for something Millfield will help you unlock it, be it electronics, art, music and of course sport. Opportunities abound at Millfield all you need do is simply show an interest and the chance would more often than not be yours.

My late father once remarked that if you could not find something to interest you at Millfield then you really have no soul and I find as I look back at my time there that this really does ring true, every taste was catered for and in a way that ensured academic studies were not neglected. Class sizes were small and with so many different sets in the A and B streams (as they were in my time), pupils found their level so as to be neither ahead or behind their peers, a truly important factor in fitting in and being accepted by classmates. No one stands out for good or bad.

I found Millfield a truly multi cultural place and an excellent grounding for life. There were so many different races, religions and cultures that there were too many to mention. Here was a school where boy from a less privileged background, perhaps on a scholarship thrown together with Princes from Africa and the Middle East and treated equally. Each learnt to understand the other and to get along and celebrate their differences, as a 13 year old boy I had my first experience of Ramadan and how children dealt with the difficulties of combining study, prayer and fasting during the hours of dawn and dusk in an environment open to the cultural nuances.

The sixty four thousand dollar question of course is would I send my own son Oscar to Millfield? The answer to this would have to be "yes" but with some caveats. While my time at the school was undoubtedly a happy experience, I do feel to really maximise your time there you need to have more than one string to your bow one of which should be "good at Sport" (although not necessarily outstanding) as you cannot escape it, sport is part of the DNA of the place. Therefore, if he turns out among other things to be a good sportsman then I know Millfield will maximise his talents and add others he never knew existed.

Mario di Monaco and Kerry Rhodes

Oakham School

Oakham

Rutland LE15 4DT

www.oakham.rutland.sch.uk

01572 758500

Andrew Crowston – Old Oakhamian (1979-1984)

OAKHAM School, founded in 1584 by Archdeacon Robert Johnson, is situated in the picturesque town of Oakham in Rutland, smack in the centre of the country, one hour 45 minutes drive from London. The school is fully co-educational with an eclectic mix of approximately 1000 pupil, 450 boarders and 550 day, with boys and girls being split equally. The school blends its 400 years history successfully with recent major modern developments that result in a truly holistic education, still based on strong Christian foundations. Solid academic achievements coupled with a strong sporting reputation places Oakham well into the first division of British public schools.

Oakham has the feel and look of a Cambridge college, quiet quads, old stone buildings over looking beautiful lawns and over 44 acres of excellent sporting grounds often used by county teams,. The campus and old school blend well together. The atmosphere is of a relaxed and happy environment where warmth, care and enthusiasm prevail enabling the school to quietly get on with implementing its ethos. The boys will be seen walking through campus and town wearing black and white tweed jackets or dark blue blazers, whilst the girls wear blazers and black and white tartan kilts. The older part of the school consists of the school chapel, recently restored, School House and Round House, where the boys and girls board for their last year. Set apart from the campus the pupils are given extra freedom and responsibility, as preparation for university life. As in my day, with prior clearance from your tutor, pupils are allowed to go the pub in the old town. Back on campus sports fields Oakham teams are increasingly beating their arch rival schools Stowe, Uppingham and Oundle. The boys and girls play in black and red sports kit.

Oakham's recent rise and success is best understood when contrasted with its rich yet mixed history. Archdeacon Robert Johnson, set up the then named "Grammar Schools" of Oakham and Uppingham in 1584. Johnson was the Puritan rector of Luffenham and Archdeacon of Leicester. He received Patronage from the William Cecil 1st Baron of Burghley and used his income from his ecclesiastical posts to set up Oakham School. As someone on the Puritan wing of the Church of England he had a strong belief in the benefits of education. In 1587 the schools endowment was confirmed by Royal Charter granted by Queen Elizabeth 1.

The original school building, still in the town centre was restored in the eighteenth century, and remained the sole classroom for over 300 years. Teaching was confined to the old school room with approx 65 boys being taught subjects including Hebrew, Latin and Greek. By 1887 the school had grown to 120 with 97 borders and 23 day boys. Whilst fortunes at Uppingham thrived during the late Victorian period, financial difficulties at Oakham followed, school numbers suffered falling to 60 odd pupils in 1905, the school was threatened with closure.

Oakham School needed to adapt and innovate. The response was to receive a grant from the local authority, and in effect become the grammar school for Rutland whilst at the same time continue as a public school. Money flowed and new facilities for science teaching, new boarding accommodation a new school house were all built. Pupil numbers began to climb reaching approx 200 by 1923. Development continued during the war period and the school added new science and language facilities. By 1970 the school had 412 boarding boys and 286 day pupils. Nowadays Oakham is one of the largest public schools in the country with approximately 460 boarders and 540 day/flexi boarding pupils. In 1970 the school became fully independent from the local authority and in 1971 took in girls for the first time, committing itself to becoming fully co-educational and becoming the first school in the country to do so with the introduction of 25 girls. Since then the school has prospered remarkably. In 1987 the school celebrated its 400 anniversary with the queen visiting.

For a school with a moderate selective intake the academic results at Oakham are very commendable and rank above some of its rivals. The most recent FT league table which measure academic performance in core subjects ranks Oakham 192, ahead of Uppingham 193, Wellington 220, Bedford School 256, and Stowe 529th.

Excellent A level results are achieved through good teaching and strong tutorial support as well as a continued focus on core subjects especially science. In 2011 58% of students achieve A or A* at A level. University success is good with 10-15 pupils gaining Oxbridge entrance. The vast majority of the remaining students head predominantly for Russell Group Universities. Most popular universities over the last 5-10 years have included: Newcastle, Leeds, Durham, Cambridge, Nottingham, UCL, Manchester and Imperial. Testament that pupils are encouraged to concentrate on core subjects at A Level. The most popular degrees being chosen for University are science based degrees. The Sciences, Mathematics and Engineering followed by Economics, History, Politics account for over 75 % of courses chosen at uni. The head, Lashbrook, recently noted that over 50% of pupils take two sciences at A levels and with the new GBP4MM Science block opening this year these trends will surely continue.

Some have might have referred to Oakham as the poorer cousin to Uppingham, but with the development in fabric and facilities implemented over the last 30 years Oakham has justifiable emerged out of the shadows of it local rivals in terms of both academic results as well as extracurricular activities, notably in sport and the arts. An Old Oakhamian (OO) recently described the key differences between Oakham and "Ping" as Oakham being perhaps, more innovative and liberal but less traditionally or formal. Whilst an Old Oakhamian who recently visited Uppingham as a possible alternative for his son thought Uppingham was looking a bit shabby and possibly losing its academic edge.

Oakham massive program of investment over the last thirty years in new infrastructure and facilities has driven it towards the top league of co-ed boarding schools. The last 5 headmasters notably Richard Bull, Smallbone,, Anthony Little (leaving Oakham to go to Eton in 2002), Spence, and currently Richard Lashbrook, all embarked on driving towards the same ethos, becoming a top co-ed boarding school in the country. This continued programme of improvement marks Oakham out from its rivals such as Uppingham, Stowe. Here a sustained history of expansion perhaps dates back to the Victorian era. Moreover, a school's recent popularity, such as Wellington, is often pinned to the arrival of a new head.

Parents are increasingly questioning future sustainable development when a headmaster's individual political ambitions lead some to question a schools continued ability to improve after departure of one reformer. The last 5 heads at Oakham have implemented and achieved what some of their rivals have been slower to implement.

New facilities continue to open including the new Mehra science block, a new GBP 4MM science block named after the Goldman Sachs partner and OO Sanjev Mehra. The new library is ranked amongst the best in the country, new dorms and houses have been opened and the existing dorms have seen significant improvements.

Investment in existing and new sporting facilities continues, new hockey pitches and tennis facilities have been added. The spectacular improvements in academic results and excellent achievements out of the class room specifically in sport, drama and music mean that Oakham is now rightly ranked as a top all round co-educational establishment.

Oakhams recent successes are naturally expanding the catchment area of the school. Pupils are increasingly coming from further afield both nationally and internationally. However, only 12 percent of pupils are international coming from Singapore, Spain, the Caribbean and Russia. Whilst the international set add to the diversity, a strong feeling of privileged middle class English set still prevails. Present day pupils are the offspring of middle class professionals such as lawyers, doctors, bankers etc. and the landed country/farming families from Lincolnshire Leicestershire Nottinghamshire which still seem to favour Oakham as they did 30 years ago.

Oakham continues to attract and develop strong all-rounders. Good sporty types will thrive and excel here with the excellent facilities and coaching on offer. The links to sporting academies of Leicestershire County Cricket and Leicester Tiger junior Rugby academy for rugby means the top flight will continue to achieve national and international standards. In 2011 Oakham reached the Daily Mail Rugby School finals at Twickenham, narrowly being beaten by Whitgift School. But, it is not just the Stuart Broads, Lewis Moodys or Tom Croft types that excel here. Sport is taken seriously by the majority with over 700 pupils playing games on any typical Wednesday. Away from sport fields the school has strength and excellence in art music and drama. The excellent Queen Elizabeth Theatre or QET offer West End standard productions. Pupils appeared in 80 musical recitals in 2011. *Et quasi cursores vitai lampada tradunt*, and, like runners, they pass on the torch of life, the school motto sums up the ethos and achievements of the school well.

Sixteen houses across the campus continue to play a significant role in school bonding. The junior school Jedwoods, has four houses, the middle school has ten six boarding and four day houses and in the final year School House and Round House cater for the final year preparations. There are usually 60-70 boys per House and Inter House rivalry in sport is strong. The head boys of School House and the head girls of Round House typically are chosen as School head boy and head girl. Privileges for head boy include growing a beard and keeping a goat! Never during my career at the school did I see a goat in Chapel Close however. School prefects known as the Decem usually 12 boys and girls are chosen by pupils and teachers during the last year and endorsed by the head master. They play a strong role in the fabric and form a link between pupils and teachers. Whilst their functions are often administrative, they are held in high esteem by their electorate pupils and the boys decem stand out in their own black and red ties.

Oakham has three routes of admission available to prospective pupils:

Firstly, into Jerwoods, the junior school at age 10-11, secondly into the middle school at 13, subject to pupils passing gaining 55% at common entrance and finally, with few pupils joining the senior school at 16.

Children entering Jerwoods will take a school examination, in January with places awarded for the following September. The school will expect pupils at this age to have command of neat written work, sound competent spelling and grammar, fluent reading and a sound basic knowledge of the primary school mathematics syllabus. Jerwoods pupils will automatically enter the Middle School and will not normally be required to sit a further examination. However, the school expects junior pupils academic attainment to be equivalent to 55% at Common Entrance requirement for entering the middle school.

For entrance into middle, the school will place great importance to the report from the Head of the pupil's prep school and a minimum grade of 55% at Common Entrance. The school notifies parents quickly usually within two weeks of the examination results. Pupils who are offered a place but defer for a year will have to re-sit the examination. For overseas pupils, the entrance procedure into middle school involves passing written papers in English and Mathematics, a diagnostic test of writing and learning skills and an interview. The school is keen to attract bright foreign students, so arrangements are made for overseas candidates to sit the examination abroad, in their home country is possible.

The sporting production line at Oakham is set to continue. Numerous recent international sports stars notably in rugby have come out of the school, in part thanks to the close links the school has forged for the top players who can train with Leicester Tigers youth development program. Lewis Moody (89-96) Tom Croft (02-04) Matt Smith (97-04), Alex Goode (04-06). Show this is working well

In cricket recent international successes include Stuart Broad 97-04. But, not to be outdone the girls are producing stars as well Lucy Pearson 83-90 England Ladies Cricket, Crista Cullen 98-03 GB Hockey and likely star at the 2012 Olympics.

In athletics, and Felicity Milton 98-05 GB Cross country GB Julian Adenniia (sp) (00-05) GB 110 MM hurdles internationalist and another Olympic hopeful. In 2011 Oakham School reached the final of the Daily Mail U18 Rugby School cup

Ian Smith, Glenn Gelderbloom and Tim Dixon-Dale the sport coaches do an excellent job in developing the schools rugby program.

Famous Old Oakhamians are increasing with national successes coming not only in sport but also across the arts as well. Mathew Mc Fayden – national actor now seen in many films, Shakespeare plays and most popularly BBC series Spooks learnt his trade at the QET. Mathew still retains links to the school and sponsors the school Inter Drama competition every year. Other OO include Greg Hicks, Katie Mitchel – Director

Music has a strong tradition at the school. Oakham School Chamber Choir recently reached the National finals as seen on TV. Peter Davis, the Schools Director of Music rightly sees this as reward and accolade for the excellent music program the school has developed.

ESTABLISHED in 1556 the school is located in Oundle, Northamptonshire approximately 65 miles north of London and 5 miles from Peterborough. Its highly attractive buildings, some dating back to the 17th century, are scattered throughout the pretty market town from which it takes its name. The town of Oundle with a population of only 6000 is greatly influenced by the school community and is to a large degree the School's campus. Pupils have the freedom and opportunity to utilise the shops and other facilities without straying far from their classrooms or Houses. Oundle is now the third largest independent boarding and day school in England with 850 boarders and 230 day pupils. The school became co-educational in 1990 and girls constitute 40% of the 1100 pupils who are accommodated in eight boys' houses, five girls' houses, one day house and one junior house.

Up until a hundred years ago Oundle was a relatively unknown grammar school for local people. However, with the arrival in 1892 of its most famous headmaster F.W. Sanderson the school rapidly expanded and soon established itself as one of England's leading public schools with a reputation in science and engineering. This reputation continues to the present day and Oundle is a highly sought after school attracting pupils from 130 prep schools throughout the land. Many families from London and the South East are beginning to view Oundle as an attractive co-educational alternative to the likes of Eton, Harrow or Radley. This is hardly surprising since nowadays Oundle is regarded as a top drawer educational establishment with a national and international reputation for academic, music and sporting excellence. Pupils are expected to work hard and the teaching is reputed to be of the highest standard. Academic results are highly impressive and approximately 25 pupils (16%) per year win places at Oxbridge. The rest head for other top universities of which the most popular are: Bristol, Durham, Edinburgh, Imperial, Leeds, Newcastle, Nottingham and UCL. A-Level results are extremely good and in 2011 the Financial Times A-Level Performance table which concentrates mainly on the more academic subjects, placed Oundle 40th just behind Harrow at 39th but well ahead of some comparable co-ed schools such as Marlborough at 76th, Rugby 172nd, Oakham 192nd, Uppingham 193rd, Haileybury 199th and Wellington 220th.

Oundle is definitely not a school for slackers but on the other hand, as one old boy put it to me, it is not an "exam factory" either. The pace of life can be frantic at this school with sport, music and lots of extra-curricular activities piled on top of a demanding academic programme. However, one need not despair. There are numerous opportunities to socialise with friends and the nurturing house system at Oundle allows everyone to return to their houses at meal times and generally "chill out". The House system is an important part of the school ethos and includes dining in the house. Boarding houses are divided into Town and Field. Town houses converted from private residences front onto the town central streets and have extensive grounds at the rear. The Field houses on the other hand are purpose built and as the name implies are located among the sports pitches a short distance from the centre. The boarding houses tend to differ in terms of character and traditions and as one would expect with such a system a healthy rivalry exists between them. Each house accommodates approximately 60 pupils with the exception of Laxton the day house which houses about 250 pupils. All pupils, regardless of faith, are expected to attend chapel three times a week and the school maintains strong links with the Church of England.

Children join Oundle at 11, 13 and a few at Sixth Form level. Approximately 40 pupils join at age 11 and they are housed in the junior boarding house, Berrystead, where they remain for two years before transferring at 13 to a senior house. Most pupils join the school at 13+ via the Common Entrance Examination (with a minimum of 55% in Maths, Science, English and French) or Oundle's own entrance exam. Sixth Form entry is by competition with only a handful of boys and girls being admitted. Most of these pupils will have achieved As or A*s in most of their GCSE subjects. It's a good idea to register at least three to four years before entry so as not to be disappointed. There are a good number of scholarships which are competed for and awarded on merit. Bursaries are also available in cases of proven need and may be up to 100% of the fees. For further information on this subject please contact the Registrar or the school website. As one would expect, the excellent all round education on offer at this school does not come cheaply. Boarding fees are £28,590 and day fees £18,480. I suppose one can console oneself with the fact that the boarding fees at Oundle are some £2000 per annum less than one would shell out for Eton or Harrow!

Unlike some other co-ed public schools where girls parade around in mini- skirts, the ladies at Oundle are modestly attired in dark navy striped culottes with a navy blazer, white blouse, navy knee length socks and black leather shoes. Boys have the more common grey trousers, navy blazer, white or blue and white striped shirt with their house or school tie. Whenever I have encountered pupils from Oundle they have rarely failed to impress me with their understated confidence, politeness and positive attitude. Naturally, these young boys and girls are intelligent enough to appreciate that they are part of an expensive and elite educational establishment which is only accessible to a tiny minority. They are privileged and they known it. However, compared with many of the alumni one encounters at some high profile public schools in the South East, Oundle pupils come across as refreshingly down to earth and are not generally regarded as arrogant or pompous.

During the 2011 Easter break I took my family to Vale do Lobo in the Algarve and enrolled my two young boys into the local tennis academy located less than 50 yards from our villa. To my surprise pupils from Oundle and two other major English public schools were present at the same tennis club. Throughout our seven day stay in Portugal this fortuitous encounter provided me with the ideal opportunity to observe at close hand the way these youngsters conducted themselves both on and off the courts. By the end of the week it had become abundantly clear to us that the Oundle set were not only good at tennis but also impeccably well behaved and good mannered. This is not to say that pupils from the other two schools were troublesome or ill mannered in any way. It is just that the Oundle representatives made a more positive impression on us.

As I mentioned earlier there is a strong sporting tradition at Oundle and the school generally performs well in rugby, cricket and hockey. There is a strong sporting rivalry with nearby Uppingham and Oakham as well as schools slightly further afield such as Harrow, Radley, Rugby and Haileybury. Rugby is played with great passion at this school and the game remains very popular. Apparently, when the 1st XV play at home, a large number of pupils turn up to cheer the team. Oundle is one of a handful of English public schools capable of fielding up to six rugby teams at senior level. Cricket is also played to a high standard and the "Ramblers" cricket team which tours throughout the U.K has acquired legendary status. Parents need to be aware that in general all sporting activities at Oundle are taken seriously and played to a high standard. The music department is housed in the old Georgian Rectory now the Gascoigne Building and has a "music for all" philosophy as their fundamental principle. 700 pupils learn a musical instrument and an astonishing 900 individual lessons are taught each week. Participation counts whether it is in one of the schools large orchestras, chapel choir or a smaller ensemble.

With the collapse of the American bank Lehman Brothers and the subsequent financial turmoil that followed, a number of private schools have seen their numbers decline. Happily this has not been the case at Oundle and the school continues to be a popular destination for ambitious parents seeking a first class education for their sons or daughters. Interestingly, not so long ago this school had the reputation of being a suitable repository for the smart families of East Anglia but, London and Home County dwellers seemed reluctant to venture up the A1 towards Peterborough. This after all is the East Midlands! Thankfully, this is no longer the case as Lawyers, City workers and other professionals who have decamped from London to the rural counties of Cambridgeshire, Huntingdonshire and Bedfordshire have discovered the charming qualities of this school and are eager to share their views with their metropolitan friends.

We live in the Hertfordshire/Buckinghamshire border which has many excellent public schools less than 50 minutes away by car. Oundle, which is a good 90 minute drive from our homes, could quite easily belong to another world. However, this is most definitely not how many feel about this school. We are personally acquainted with a number of families who reside a mere stone throw from the M25 who have been highly impressed with Oundle and have chosen to send their offspring here in preference to schools nearer home. Clearly they have seen the merits of an Oundle education and are quite prepared to travel the extra miles.

In summary, an excellent co-educational establishment firmly embedded within the top stratus of our major public schools. Oundle is a top notch school which deserves to be viewed as a serious player. As one young lady in Rock, Cornwall, told me this summer: Eton and Harrow may still rule the roost, but Radley, Rugby and Oundle are not far behind.

RADLEY COLLEGE

Abingdon

Oxfordshire OX14 2HR

www.radley.org.uk

01235 543127

FOUNDED in 1847, this traditional educational establishment with around 690 pupils is situated some 5 miles from Oxford and by all accounts retains many of the charming characteristics of the quintessential English public school. In common with Eton, Harrow and Winchester it has managed to resist the temptations of co-education, or day pupils and has remained a boys' only full boarding school.

Radley has always been a desirable school but, since it featured in a series of television programmes for the B.B.C. in 1979, it has experienced a rise in popularity of stellar proportions. Many ambitious families will now look to Radley as a suitable alternative to Eton. Proof of this can be found on the web sites of a number of famous country preps such as Ludgrove, Summer Fields or Cothill. Having said that, it would be wrong to assume that Radley has become a repository for would be Etonians who have failed to make the grade. This school has its own unique appeal and an increasing number of boys capable of winning places at Eton are doing what not so long ago would have been "unthinkable". They are opting for Radley as their first choice!

Radley may be fashionable and in great demand, but assuming that you know how to go about it, gaining entry is neither fiendishly difficult nor super selective. The school operates a somewhat antiquated but very fair and seemingly successful admissions policy based on a first come first served system. If you drag your feet and attempt to register when your son is well into his prep school years, you are likely to be disappointed. To secure a place at Radley you must act early before the list is closed. Many prospective parents now apply soon after birth and in some cases fathers have been known to ring the school from the labour ward! Once you have successfully completed the application process you can relax. There after subject to a satisfactory prep school report, so long as your son obtains an average of 60% in the Common Entrance exam, there should not be any problems. For those parents who have discovered Radley late there is a small lifeline available in the form of the Warden's (Headmaster) List. This list allows entry into the school to a small number of unregistered boys with talents in the arts or sports who have been recommended by their Prep school Headmasters and who achieve the required minimum in the Common Entrance. In addition, around 20 scholarships are awarded each year and candidates can apply for academic, art, music, drama or all rounder awards.

Regardless of its popularity this famous institution, like all others, does have the odd critic. The amusing "rah-rah Radley" label appears to have gained momentum and the school is still perceived by some as a Sloaney outfit lacking racial diversity. To a degree this is probably true and few would argue that this strong Church of England school is a popular choice for upper middle class protestant British families who generally, but not exclusively, reside in the South of England. However, the most plausible explanation as to why so few non indigenous boys end up at Radley, is probably because many overseas parents are unlikely to be acquainted with the schools unique but totally non discriminatory entry system requiring early registration. By the time Radley comes onto the radar of families from beyond our shores, it is often too late to register and their only options are the few places available through the Wardens List.

For a mixed ability school with a moderately selective intake Radley, achieves phenomenally good academic results. The Oxbridge success rate is between 15%-18% and the rest end up at highly rated Universities such as Bristol, Durham, Edinburgh, Newcastle, Leeds, St Andrews and UCL to mention the most popular. A-Level results are highly impressive and achieved by hard work and excellent teaching. By and large the boys are encouraged to concentrate on the harder more traditional A-level subjects at the expense of "softer" choices so as not to jeopardise their chances of gaining access to our top universities. Moreover, unlike many other private schools who reputedly throw out candidates likely to spoil their overall A-Level results Radley, does not weed out weak pupils after GCSEs. High flyers and trailing edges are in it together for the full five years. Naturally, parents find this very reassuring, but, one can only wonder how much further up the academic tables Radley would be if progression into the sixth form was selective. That said, the school does not do too badly. In 2011 the Financial Times League Tables for

Independent Schools based on government statistics, ranked Radley 23rd, behind Winchester 7th and Eton 13th, but ahead of Harrow 39th, Marlborough 76th, Wellington 220th, St Edward's 480th and Stowe 520th.

As stated earlier all the boys at Radley are full boarders. They are accommodated in Houses known as Socials which are known by a letter A-K. Each Social aims to accommodate 65-70 boys and no more than three boys from any one Prep school. To quote a senior master "boys come to Radley and not to a particular Social". The school actively ensures that all the Socials have a good mix of boys with diverse talents". In 2008 two new Socials, J and K were added to the school and despite their lack of tradition, the extra space and modern facilities have proved popular. By the way no formal uniform exists at this school. Pupils wear the famous black Radley gown over suits, blazers and tweed jackets.

As one would expect from a school set in 800 acres of idyllic Oxfordshire countryside and attended largely by boys from traditional English homes, field sports are well catered for. Despite the hunting ban introduced by the last Labour government, the Beagling Pack remains and boys are encouraged to exercise and look after the Beagles. Clay pigeon shooting is popular and for those who enjoy fly-fishing there is a lake stocked with trout. The school also keeps pigs. For those who take sports seriously this is the ideal school. Keen rugby players, potential county cricketers or "wet bobs" who dream of winning the Princess Elizabeth Cup at Henley will not be disappointed. It has been ten years since the rowers lifted this trophy but the school always seem to manage a semi-final or at the very least a quarter-final place. In 2011 Radley were beaten in the semis by their neighbours and rowing rivals Abingdon in a race which Olympic gold medallist Sir Mathew Pinsett, described as one of the best he had seen from school boys. Abingdon went on to win the cup defeating an American school in the final. Rugby is almost a religion at Radley and played with passion against other top schools such as Eton,

Harrow, Sherborne and Oundle but interestingly not against Wellington College. Many famous cricketers have attended this great school and of course Radley old boy Andrew Strauss is the present captain of the England cricket team. It doesn't get much better than this! For those who enjoy golf the school offers a Par 3, 4 and 5 nine-hole golf course. In general all sporting facilities are excellent at Radley and a newly built Real Tennis court adds to the outstanding choices available. Radley extensive grounds include game pitches which are reputed to have the longest continuous area of mown grass in the south of England.

Whereas many parents are attracted to the splendid isolation and campus nature of this school, one or two have rather unflatteringly described it as a monastery. Parents are of course entitled to express their views, but, in my opinion Radley is most certainly not detached from the real world. Its close proximity to Oxford ensures that boys (with permission and supervision) can pop over to utilise many of the facilities

available within this vibrant and cultural city. Also Oxford University Dons frequently come to Radley to give lectures to the boys. Social events with girls' schools ensure that the boys have plenty of opportunities to mingle with young ladies from Downe House, Tudor Hall, Wycombe Abbey, Cheltenham Ladies College and the nearby St Katherine and St Helen's School. Rather provocatively, I have heard that Downe House girls generally find Radley boys more attractive than Etonians!

One of the most striking features about Radley College is the strength and depth of its art department. The school most definitely excels in this subject and high quality works of art are on display throughout the school. The exceptional artistic talents of many of the boys made a lasting impression on us when we visited Radley. The Performing Arts too are strong, helped by the state-of-the-art new theatre in which a striking performance of Sweeny Todd in 2011 drew great acclaim and it was no surprise that the lead actor has since been offered a place at The Central

School of Speech and Drama. Music is also popular and most boys play more than one instrument. A particular feature is the impressive Chapel Choir with a treble line of choristers drawn from local primary and prep schools. The magnificent chapel with it famous stained glass is revered by many and attendance is compulsory five times per week. Also attractive is the spacious dining room which bears a striking resemblance to the one at Hogwarts School of Magic, Harry Potter's Alma Mater!

Thanks to old Radleian Andrew Strauss leading England to a victorious Ashes win against Australia, the school has had a fair amount of positive publicity of late. Radley is also now represented at government level by old boy Owen Patterson who sits in David Cameron's Cabinet. Andrew Motion the former Poet Laureate is also a product of this rounded school. Many old boys seem to end up in the City, the professions or the smarter army regiments. The world of property especially upmarket firms such as Knight Franks also attracts a fair number.

Radley has been riding high for many years and some of its rivals are wondering when the bubble will burst. Judging from what we hear about this school, parents are still extremely keen to educate their sons at Radley, so it is unlikely that the school will suffer any meaningful decline in the near future. Like Eton, Radley quietly gets on with the business of educating boys without the need to advertise in glossy magazines or purchase stands at independent schools shows in London. Discretion is clearly the name of the game at Radley and I for one can't recall ever seeing an advertisement about this school anywhere! As one prep school headmaster recently told me, Radley, does not need to indulge in hard sell. Families who have sons at famous prep schools such as Ludgrove, Cothill, Summer Fields, Caldicott, Aysgarth, Dragon etc. will know all that one needs to know about Radley.

In summary an outstanding and traditional public school that has effortlessly managed to blend the old with the new. Its rounded alumni are on the whole polite, considerate and self assured. We are highly impressed with what this place has to offer and would recommend it to any one searching for a single sex full boarding school.

ROEDEAN SCHOOL

Brighton

Sussex BN2 5RQ

www.roedean.co.uk

01273 667500

ROEDEAN School stretches grandly along the blustery South Downs and the views if not the wind will take your breath away! Set in 120 acres and bordering the South Downs National Park the school was founded in 1885 by the Lawrence sisters; Penelope, Millicent and Dorothy, their aim was to offer girls the same level of education enjoyed by their brothers. The initial purpose was to prepare girls for Newnham and Girton Colleges at Cambridge. Known as "The Firm" the Lawrences were joined in 1897 by Katherine Earle who in 1903 set sail for South Africa with Theresa Lawrence where they established Roedean in Parktown, Johannesburg as a school for the "daughters of the colonies". It still stands today as the best girls school in South Africa.

A small school, mainly boarding and with just under 400 pupils, the personal interaction between staff and children is really evident here. Girls are accommodated in four houses dependant on year groups. The younger girls share bedrooms with friends until the Fifth Form when individual study bedrooms are provided. In March 2012 the school embarked upon complete refurbishment of the boarding houses, a lengthy project but now well underway. A firm of architects, known for their designs of boutique hotels, will be stripping back and reinstating the original Art and Crafts features. It has recently been announced that from September 2012 weekly and flexi-boarding will be offered, largely due to demand from parents living in London and the South East.

Facilities for sport, music, art, theatre and of course teaching are truly cutting edge. Girls excel in all sports of which 30 are offered. Netball and Lacrosse are particularly strong and the Centenary sports hall would easily meet the standards of an upmarket health club. 12 tennis courts overlook the sea but during inclement weather squash, badminton and trampolining are popular. The theatre seats 320 and is of a professional standard and can be hired out commercially. An exquisite chapel adds to the spiritual life of the school and girls are encouraged to explore their own faith and indeed learn about and understand the faiths of others.

In the past a Roedean girl would have been educated and groomed to be the perfect CEO's wife. Nowadays they are far more likely to be the CEO themselves. 58% of 2011 leavers have gone on to their first choice of university to study science, technology, engineering and mathematics. STEM courses as they are known have long led to male dominated professions and to see such vast numbers of girl entering fields such as these is indicative not only of social change but also in the way that these subjects are taught. Ranked 158 by the Financial times Independent Schools league table, A-Level results are good with 77% obtaining A*-B grades but bearing this in mind the number of girls going to Oxford, Cambridge or UCL was an impressive 13% in 2011. This compares very favourably with similar schools like Benenden who have a 14% Oxbridge entry, Downe House with 15% but not quite to the level of Cheltenham Ladies College with 26%. However the large majority of Old Roedeanians are taking up places at the next tier of prestigious universities such as Bristol, University College London, Warwick and the London School of Economics. Some girls are spreading their wings even further to the American Ivy League institutions.

In 2009 Roedean took over the ailing St Mary's Hall school, most of those girls merged into Roedean at the age of 11 or 13. The subsequent sale of buildings has created a substantial endowment fund in excess of £10 million. This will provide ongoing means tested bursaries. The eventual aim is to be able to offer around 10% of girls a full bursary. As St Mary's Hall was founded in 1836 to educate the daughters of poor Clergymen a number of bursaries are still offered to those meeting that criteria. There are, of course, the usual raft of scholarships available for girls who excel in the arts, sport or academia. There is one particular award however which is very much worth mentioning. The Brighthelm Award offers full tuition and boarding as well as an additional sum to cover uniforms and school trips. As any private school parent is aware these "thrills and spills" certainly add up. The Brighthelm is only available to local girls who live within 20 miles of Brighton, only three award holders may be at the school at any one time which makes this award extremely prestigious.

Roedean is probably one of the most well known girls' schools in the country. But beyond all the facts and figures it has, as old girls or parents will tell you, an indefinable quality, a connection with tradition , that little something extra which makes it a very special place to educate your daughters.

Mario di Monaco with Kerry Rhodes

RUGBY SCHOOL

Rugby

Warwickshire CV22 5EH

www.rugbyschool.net

01788 556216

FOUNDED in 1567 Rugby is justifiably renowned as one of our most famous public schools. Together with Eton, Harrow, Winchester, Shrewsbury, Charterhouse, Westminster, St Paul's and Merchant Taylors it formed part of the Public Schools Act of 1868 which was enacted to regulate and reform the nine leading boys' schools of the time. Located in the town of Rugby, in Warwickshire (the heart of England) the schools buildings, a mixture of traditional houses and cutting edge classroom technology, dominate the town centre. Such convenient location served by excellent rail and road links has made Rugby a national school with pupils coming from every corner of the British Isles.

Modern day Rugby is a co-educational school which also provides for a small number of day pupils. Out of a total of 800 alumni approximately 140 are day and the rest are full boarders which at Rugby means exactly that i.e. no sloping off home on Saturday afternoons except for exeat weekends. At present the gender ratio is 57% boys and 43% girls thus creating a fairly balanced co-educational environment. Both sexes are required to wear the traditional uniform which consists of tweed jackets and grey trousers for boys and in the case of girls similar tweed jackets and very long, almost down to the ankles, grey skirts. Apparently a perennial discussion takes place on the subject of skirts length.

Modernisers within the school are pushing for girls skirts to be made shorter so that they can project a more feminine image!

Rugby is an exciting place to study and a number of educationalists acquainted with private education regard this place as probably the best co-educational boarding school in England. That said, the school is most definitely not an exam factory, or overrun by academic superstars. The schools ethos is to challenge bright pupils who are destined for the top universities whilst at the same time encourage less academically minded souls to achieve good results which often exceed expectations. Pupils can study for the traditional A-Levels or take the Cambridge Pre-U which Rugby played an instrumental part in the development of this examination. It has to be said that for a mixed ability school academic results at Rugby are quite exceptional. In 2011 the Oxbridge "hit rate" was astonishingly high at 16%, which is considerably higher than most of its co-educational competitors. Other popular universities seem to be U.C.L., Durham, Bristol, Leeds, Manchester, Exeter, St Andrews and Edinburgh. Medicine at U.C.L is apparently a desirable destination for those with scientific attributes. As for A-Level results, according to the Financial Times Independent Schools League Tables the A*- B grades came in at 84% placing Rugby at 172nd on the list. Compared with other co-ed schools Rugby fared less well than Oundle (40th) and Marlborough (76th) but better than Uppingham (193rd), Oakham (192nd), Wellington (220th) St Edwards Oxford (483rd) and Stowe (529).

Admission to Rugby is competitive but not fiendishly difficult. There are three points of entry to this school. Age 11+ which is open only to day pupils from maintained schools or independent schools that finish at 11. At 13+ you need to register for a house and visit three to four years in advance. Around 18 months prior to admission you will need to take the computerized test, be interviewed by the housemaster or mistress as well as another senior staff member. In addition a detailed report from the current head of your son/daughter's prep school will be requested. Once these assessments have taken place offers are made conditional to obtaining 55% in the Common Entrance Examination or Rugby's own exam should your school not prepare for Common Entrance. The vast majority of the pupils come to Rugby at the 13+ stage but a handful also join the school at 16+ for entry into the Sixth Form. There is practically no "culling" after GCSEs as progression into the Sixth Form only requires candidates to obtain a very modest 5 Bs at GCSEs. As is the case at most other top public schools the fees at Rugby are staggeringly high. Annual day fees range from £18 000 - £23 000 and annual boarding fees are in excess of £28 000.

The social standing of a particular public school still seems to matter to a significant number of parents. Some places have a reputation for being "posh", others are known for being more down to earth. Never underestimate the social class factor which in my opinion remains an important issue for some parents. Rugby of course has always been renowned as an exclusive, elite and desirable school and although it has lost some of its former prominence it is still up there with the very best. However one of the housemasters I spoke to when we visited the school was at pains to stress that pupils at Rugby come from a wide variety of backgrounds and the school aims to reflect this diversity in what it offers and how it promotes itself. The implication was that Rugby is not as socially exclusive as Eton or Harrow. This intriguing comparison was not totally unexpected. Those of you who are familiar with the latest version of "Brideshead Revisited" will recall a scene in the film when the Old Etonian aristocratic Sebastian Flyte introduces his new friend Charles Ryder to a gaggle of fellow Etonians sipping champagne before lunch at an Oxford College. One of the more vocal members of the group announced that he couldn't remember Charles at Eton. Sebastian's reply was that Charles had been educated elsewhere without actually naming the school. This ambiguity was clearly not good enough for the old Etonians who unashamedly continued to probe. If not Eton they asked, had he attended Harrow perhaps, or possibly Winchester or maybe Rugby? The answer was never made clear but, the implications most certainly were. In the closeted world of Oxford University circa 1930's Rugby, it seems, was part of a small number of schools deemed suitable alternatives to Eton.

Rugby School became deeply embedded in the national psyche towards the end of the 19th Century with the appointment of the schools most notable Headmaster Thomas Arnold in 1828. During his 14 year period at the helm he executed many reforms to the curriculum and administration and was immortalized in Thomas Hughes book "Tom Brown's School Days". Fiction apart, the legacy that Arnold left behind provided an educational model which was soon adopted by other public schools. Rugby's influence during and soon after Arnold's tenure was far reaching and in many ways the stereotype of the quintessential English public school is to a large degree a re-working of Thomas Arnold's Rugby.

Naturally, there have been many changes to this school since Tom Brown's school days but, the principles of the charismatic and revolutionary Arnold have certainly not all been confined to history. The school proudly boasts 32 Arnold Foundation Bursaries which are open to boys and girls from underprivileged backgrounds. These bursaries are means tested and if necessary can cover up to 110% of the school fees (the extra 10% is designed to cover the cost of uniforms, music lessons, travelling expenses etc). The Arnold Foundation Bursaries are extremely generous and it is highly commendable for a school like Rugby to open its exclusive doors so widely to a very large number of deserving pupils who under normal circumstances would never have the opportunity for such an education.

As stated earlier Rugby is predominantly a full boarding school with a full range of activities taking place on Sundays. The pupils are allowed to go into town in groups but they are prohibited from venturing out beyond a perimeter designated by the school. According to a couple of boys I quizzed on this subject, they are not allowed into the "grotty parts". Amusingly, this prompted a spontaneous riposte from a teacher who stated that Rugby had no grotty parts! Anyhow, this should not be a major issue for parents. The schools striking redbrick buildings are located in the genteel town centre and the surrounding shops and cafes provide a welcome outlet for pupils to stay in touch with "the real world". That said, it is debatable whether someone who attends an elite boarding school can ever truly understand the so called real world. The Labour politician John Prescott, former deputy Prime Minister, filmed part of his television programme on Class at Rugby school and by all accounts made his negative views on public schools of this nature abundantly clear. He seemed to imply that it is all very well offering fully funded bursaries to children from working class homes and provide them with a private education. However, by the time they had left Rugby he argued, most of them would have abandoned their roots and finish up in a world of privilege a million miles from their former homes. This of course is absolutely correct and clearly demonstrates how social mobility can transform lives. But is there anything wrong with this? One may be born into a humble home in an industrial town, but if he or she qualifies as a doctor or lawyer, irrespective of where they have been educated, they are hardly likely to return to their terraced house and resume normal relationships with their families or old friends.

There are 15 Houses at Rugby of which eight are for boys and seven for girls. Two of the Houses are day houses, Town House for boys and Southfield House for girls. Stanley House, an ex boys house, now accommodates Sixth Form girls only. Naturally, there is a resident Housemaster or mistress, along with a deputy, matron and tutors. Each child maintains the same tutor throughout senior school which allows for continuity of care. Accommodation starts in small dormitories and by the sixth form pupils are in single bedrooms. As it is often the case in traditional boarding schools, some Houses are more popular than others and an unofficial pecking order appears to exist. The conveniently located School Field and School House are reputedly the most desirable with Michell House also in demand. School Field is the oldest house and its location bang in the middle of the school provides spectacular views for the 55 boys who reside there. The charming housemaster Dr Beesley (educated at Repton), kindly showed us around the house and particularly attractive was the dining room which resembled a miniature version of the one at Hogwarts. By the way there is no central eating at Rugby and the pupils all dine in their own houses. The housemasters/mistresses, whenever possible, eat all the meals with their pupils. During our visit we were also shown Michell House which has a very strong sporting tradition. Though less quaint than School Field we were made to feel most welcome by the enthusiastic Housemaster Tim Day (Old Rugbeian) and we most certainly enjoyed our lunch in their cosy dining room accompanied by the boys. Sipping coffee in the reception room with the Housemasters and his wife surrounded by children's toys, made this house feel particularly homely.

As one would expect from a school with a strong Anglican foundation, frequent services are held in the strikingly beautiful large chapel which can accommodate all of the 800 pupils at the same time. Chapel is central to the school's spiritual and moral philosophies as set out by its most well known Headmaster Dr Thomas Arnold well over 130 years ago. The pastoral care at Rugby is deemed to be excellent by many and pupils in general feel well looked after. There is "zero tolerance" on bullying and "words can hurt, think about what you say" posters were seen throughout the school. Senior students are encouraged to help younger ones to find their feet and allow mutual respect to flourish in a stable and caring environment.

The game of Rugby owes its name to the school and not surprisingly boys are keen to display their skills against the likes of Radley, Oundle and Uppingham. However, with the school being fully co-educational, the stock of potential players has steadily diminished and the school is not quite the force it once was on the rugby fields. The legend of William Webb Ellis and the origin of the game is commemorated by a plaque. It is also widely believed that cross country running began at this school and the Crick Run which started in 1838 is still a major annual event in the school's calendar.

In summary, an excellent co-educational school with a fine pedigree and a long list of famous Alumni such as the poet Rupert Brooks, Prime Minister Neville Chamberlain, Lewis Carroll, the author Salman Rushdie, and the so called father of the sport of rugby William Webb Ellis to mention but a few of the great people who have been educated at this school.

Please read on and find out what a mother and daughter have to say about Rugby school:

Life as a Rugby School pupil

Having moved from a girls' day school to a mixed boarding school for sixth form last year, I found the transition, at least to begin with, rather unnerving. Rugby was very different to my previous school, however I immediately found myself thrown into a whirlwind of different activities, clubs, outings and other events. With my occasionally disorganised personality, I really benefit from the structure of our daily routine: for example specific times for meals, prep etc.; but we also have free time during the week and on the weekend. For example Tuesday and Thursday afternoons are set aside for sports and activities (usually community-based) respectively.

The boarding house plays a particularly central role to each pupil's school life. I particularly appreciated this at the beginning, going into the only girls' sixth form house, i.e. where everyone was new at the time and the focus was therefore mainly on us! In the lower sixth (or "Lower Twenty – LXX") you are assigned a big "sister" to guide you and answer any questions, and your housemaster/ mistress, deputy and tutor also helps you in any way they can. I have also made friends with people from so many different backgrounds, as a result of a very sociable lifestyle at school. On Saturdays, "bar" is usually organised, at which we are allowed two alcoholic drinks and a DJ is hired. This is in addition to things such "stodge" (i.e. tuck shop); "Bluenote" (another social event in which people play music); or otherwise visiting each others' houses each weekday evening after prep.

Overall, I did find myself in a slightly, but not overwhelmingly, more masculine environment, particularly in lessons, but I found it was much more balanced compared to my previous school, which was at times very "clique"-orientated. And so far, male presence hasn't distracted me from my studies! The school are very encouraging towards hard work, as part of a "well-rounded" school career which of course involves learning other skills and taking part in music, acting, sports and so on. We also have the chance to take part in trips, from house-organised outings to the nearby bowling alley to geography field trips to Barcelona or a French Business Conference in Paris, depending on the subjects you choose.

...and a little insight from a new parent...

Isabel's house (Stanley House) is a house of approx. 50 sixth form girls, all of whom are new to the school. All meals are cooked in house so offering true "home cooking". The food is excellent offering decent quantities and lots of vegetarian and salad type options.

As a parent I feel that girls are felt to be an integral part of the school and now that they are just about 50 per cent of pupils, there is no difference in the way girls and boys are treated.

As Isabel says, the house is the centre of school life. The house does its own "team building" outings especially at the beginning of the year and holds an annual house ball to which boys and girls from other houses are invited. Girls are protected from "gawping" – Mrs Shelley doesn't like boys coming into the house to inspect her new girls.

Most weekends the school holds "bar" – a gathering of sixth form boys and girls which often has a fancy dress theme. A small quantity of alcohol WITH THE MEAL is permitted for 17 year olds.

Overall, the kids seem to work hard – Isabel is working harder than she did before going to Rugby, and have a lot of fun. Reluctant teenagers are pushed into doing some sport. Television is not watched very much and they do loads of activities – so much so you are warned your child is likely to be "on their knees" with exhaustion by term end!

SHERBORNE SCHOOL

Sherborne

Dorset DT9 3AP

www.sherborne.org

01935 810402

THIS very old and traditional public school is situated in the delightful town of Sherborne in Dorset. For parents who wish to educate their sons in a single sex full boarding school, Sherborne provides an attractive alternative to the likes of Eton, Winchester, Harrow and Radley. Some of the architecturally striking buildings, such as School House date back to the 17th century, but the school can trace its origins to the 8th century when it was linked with the Benedictine Abbey in the town. After the dissolution of the monasteries, the school was refounded by Edward VI in 1550 as a free grammar school for local boys. Since then the school has undergone many changes and modern day Sherborne is a first division public school renowned throughout Britain. It has certainly raised its profile to new heights over the last decade and now forms part of an exclusive group of Sloaney schools whose pupils are frequently encountered along the Cornish beaches of Rock and Polzeath during the summer months.

There are 600 boys at Sherborne of which 548 are full boarders. The handful of day pupils at the school are fully integrated into one of the 8 boarding Houses and have beds allocated to them which they can use whenever they wish. From a practical perspective, Sherborne has to be viewed as a full boarding school where boys are only allowed home on exeats weekends and half term. This place is most definitely not a "Bread and Breakfast" educational establishment like some of the public schools in the south east of England. Here there is no going home after Saturday afternoon activities. Also, possibly because the school is a fair distance from London and its international airports, there are only 33 boys from overseas at the school at this present time. As for choosing a House, like all traditional boarding schools, some Houses are more popular than others, and often their popularity changes with time. I have been reliably informed that at present the two Houses which fill up quickly are Digby and School House. Boarding fees at £ 29,175 are very much in line with other top drawer public schools. Parents generally come from the West Country and the majority live no more than 90 minutes from the school. An increasing number are coming from London and the south east and if they do not relish the longish drive, Sherborne can be reached by rail from Waterloo.

Sherborne is a moderately selective school and admission at 13+ is via the Common Entrance Examination, where a minimum of 55% is required. There is no official closing date for registering your son and in theory one can apply quite late; although this is not advisable as the list may be closed for a particular year if it becomes oversubscribed. The usual scholarships are offered and in addition to the coveted academic ones, awards are also available in music, art, sport and D.T. Mean tested bursaries are also available. Sixth Form entry is limited to approximately 20 boys and a pass in Sherborne's own entrance papers as well as a minimum of 5 GCSEs at grade B or above is required to secure a place. The school offers the usual list of popular A-levels and for those seeking a broader curriculum the I.B. is available. The latter is taught in classes shared with young ladies from the nearby Sherborne Girls School. This of course, means that in the Sixth Form some of the classes are co-educational. Many parents seem to be relaxed about this and welcome the introduction of mixed classes at this fairly mature stage.

Academic results are good and last year the average I.B. score was a highly commendable 35 points per candidate. A-level results however, were less impressive with the A* A and B pass rate coming in at a modest 69% lower than the 76% achieved in 2010. The 2011 Financial Times Tables for Independent Schools, ranked Sherborne 316 which is some way down from Radley 23rd, Marlborough 76th and Wellington 220th.However, the school fared better than Bradfield 401, Bryanston 450, and Stowe 529. The Oxbridge success rate was a satisfactory 7%. Reading between the lines, it seems that the brighter boys are opting for the I.B. which makes academic comparisons with other schools a complex business.

Sport at Sherbone is a big thing and the school main winter game is rugby. This is played to an extremely high level and needle matches against rivals Radley, Marlborough, Wellington and Bryanston are always well supported. I n 1991 a pupil at the school wrote "A History of Rugby at Sherborne School" an account of the intimate relationship the school has had with the game for more than a century. Cricket is also played passionately and to a high standard. The school's cricket ground, the Upper, is used by the first XI and the ground is also one of the venues used by Dorset for their home fixtures. The major sports are rugby in the Michaelmas term, Hockey in the Lent term and cricket in the Trinity term. There is no rowing at Sherbone. However, lots of other sporting activities are on offer. These include: Football, polo, swimming, shooting, golf, fencing, sailing, windsurfing and many more. Sport is seen as an important component of school life and with 50 acres of playing fields accommodating 17 matches at any one time, every boy can take part and see his abilities develop.

Music is held in high esteem at this school and perhaps the most popular aspect is the Rock Society, often referred to as "Roc Soc", run by the boys and supported by expert staff. They put on concerts every term and the biggest is the "Concerts in the Courts" which is open to all the school including its sister school Sherbone Girls as well as enthusiastic fans from a clutch of other schools. When it comes to Drama, this school truly excels. It is no coincidence that some of Britain's most accomplished names of film and theatre such as Hugh Bonneville, Jeremy Irons, Richard Eyre and John Le Mesurier were all educated at Sherbone. All aspect of performance and theatre production are taken very seriously at Sherborne and the school has been known to send successful shows to the Edinburgh Festival.

I would like to complete this article by quoting a few lines from the school's prospective which convey an important and relevant message to all parents. "We want boys to leave Sherbone feeling happy and balanced and then to remain so. In order to succeed in today's competitive society, we believe that the decisions they make about their future must be both well-researched and heart-felt. This preparation is part of their education, not an adjunct to it....the process begins as soon as they enter the school. This means that when advice about careers and further education is eventually given, it is against a solid background knowledge of each boy's personality and emerging academic strengths".

SHREWSBURY SCHOOL

The Schools

Shrewsbury, SY3 7BA

www.shrewsbury.org.uk

01743 280500

SHREWSBURY School founded in 1552 by King Edward VI, has always been one of the great public schools of England. In 1882 the school moved to its present site along the banks of the River Severn where spectacular views of the valley and beyond provide an idyllic setting for the pupils to admire. It is certainly a very pretty school set in wonderful surroundings and was recognized as one of the leading public schools by the Clarendon Commission together with other famous schools such as Eton, Winchester, Rugby, Charterhouse and Harrow that were defined by the public schools act of 1868. Shrewsbury was originally a boarding school for boys however, since 2008 girls have been admitted into the Sixth Form. There are now approximately 720 pupils at the school and from September 2014 Shrewsbury will start taking girls as well as boys into the third form.

Entry into Shrewsbury is not highly selective and this educational establishment remains a broad academic church. The school seems to have the enviable reputation of being able to attract pupils of the highest abilities as well as those who have yet to flourish or demonstrate their true potential. The school prides itself on the fact that it is quite capable of awakening dormant qualities in those who have just scraped their pass mark whilst at the same time stretch and challenge scholars who are already accomplished performers and possibly destined for our top universities. Pupils are admitted at 13+ via Common Entrance Examination and tend to come from a fairly wide range of prep schools. My son's prep school, Lockers Park in Hertfordshire, has a high degree of respect for Shrewsbury and over the years has sent a steady stream of boys to this school. Approximately 10% of the intake is made up of pupils where English is their second language. Shrewsbury may be a fair drive from London and the South East, but apparently an increasing number of parents who may be considering boys only schools such as Eton, Radley or Harrow are also looking at Shrewsbury as an attractive and suitable co-educational alternative.

Academic results are extremely good and particularly impressive is Shrewsbury's ability to get a surprisingly high number of students into Oxbridge. In 2012, 13 candidates were successful in winning places at our two most famous universities with nine going to Oxford and four to Cambridge. Furthermore, last year's A-Level results broke school records with an A*-B pass rate of 81% and a highly commendable A*-A pass rate of 56%. 13 students achieved three or more A* grades. In addition to the traditional A-Levels the school curriculum now also includes the more challenging new Cambridge Pre-U. In 2011 the Financial Times Independent Schools academic league table ranked Shrewsbury 217 which compared well with Rugby 172nd, Uppingham 193rd, Oakham 192nd, Repton 330th and Haileybury 199th. However, these comparisons must not be taken too seriously as they are merely meant to illustrate that Shrewsbury is capable of delivering academic results comparable to other well known co-ed schools with similar admission policies.

The vast majority of pupils at Shrewsbury (84%) are full boarders, and as one would expect from an old English public school, this institution is run very much along the lines of a traditional full boarding school. There are 11 boarding Houses and two day Houses at Shrewsbury with two newly built houses reserved for Sixth Form girls who can be either day girls or boarders. The other nine houses accommodate on average 60 boys and each house has a dedicated Housemaster or Housemistress supported by Matron and a team of tutors. Senior pupils are encouraged to take responsibility for the good running of the houses. The pastoral care is reputed to be of a high standard and the 10% of overseas pupils are happily integrated into the boarding community. Shrewsbury is a proper boarding school and at weekends the place is packed with activities such as sport, orchestral rehearsals, choral concerts, painting classes, visiting lectures and so on. This is unquestionably a vibrant and exciting school to attend and one can easily understand why it is such a desirable place to educate one's son or daughter.

Shrewsbury has a superb reputation in a number of sports and boys have been known to compete internationally in rowing and cricket. Talking of rowing, four years ago at the Henley Royal Regatta, we witnessed an astonishing race in the final when with the last few strokes, Shrewsbury managed to edge out a strong American school on the line to win the coveted Princess Elizabeth Cup. The whole of the Stewards Enclosure erupted once the result was announced as Etonians, Radleians, Bedfordians etc. put aside old rivalries and rejoiced in an English victory. Shrewsbury is also a strong rugby school and the game is played to a very high standard. The school also enjoys a reputation as of the best football schools in the country and one where the sport of "five" is played to a high standard. Cross country is also popular and the running club is traditionally known as The Hunt! Girls compete in hockey, netball and tennis as well as other sports such as swimming and badminton.

The school's old boys are known as "Old Salopians" and many such as the naturalist Charles Darwin and the poet Sir Philip Sidney have achieved lasting fame. Other famous alumni include: Martin Rees, President of the Royal Society and Astronomer Royal, the author Samuel Butler, broadcaster John Peel, the author Nevil Shute, journalist and founder of Private Eye Richard Ingram, former Conservative Deputy Prime Minister Michael Heseltine, broadcaster Michael Palin and Christopher Booker, co-founder of the satirical magazine Private Eye. Naturally, a school of this calibre and pedigree has many more famous old boys which could be justifiably added to this list if time and space permitted!

In conclusion, a top drawer public school set in an enviable location, albeit a fair distance from London and the south east. Parents who are prepared to brave the journey should most definitely place this school high on their list of choices. Smart families from the midlands and the north have always rated this great school and continue to do so in numbers. Shrewsbury is academically sound and exceptionally sporty. Rowers, rugby players and cricketers will not be disappointed here and soon get used to winning. Shrewsbury may no longer be the all boys educational bastion of old, however, the introduction of girls has been popular and the school is rightly or wrongly heading down the co-educational route. Will this make the school less competitive in rowing or rugby? Possibly; however, do not be surprised if they lift the Princess Elizabeth Cup again in the near future.

ST EDWARD'S OXFORD

Woodstock Road

Oxford OX2 7NN

www.stedwards.oxon.sch.uk

01865 319200

ST EDWARD'S, also colloquially known as "Teddies", is a nationally renowned co-educational school located two miles north of the city centre of Oxford where it occupies 100 acres including 90 acres of playing fields. Founded in 1863, the school was initially based in the centre of the city however, due to rapid expansion it relocated to its present site in Summertown ten years later. The attractive Victorian redbrick buildings set in a quadrangular fashion resemble a cloistered Oxford college of the same period. For many years Teddies was a well kept local secret and many of the pupils attending were from Oxfordshire, London, Berkshire and Buckinghamshire. However over the last decade or so the school has raised its profile and families from further afield are being attracted to this school.

In common with the majority of boys only boarding schools, Teddies chose to become co-educational and girls were first admitted to the Sixth Form in 1982. The school became fully co-ed in 1997 and in 1999 Holly Branson, daughter of Sir Richard Branson became the first ever Head of School. Holly went on to read medicine at university and qualified as a doctor. St Edward's is predominantly a boarding school and out of a total of 670 pupils 512 are boarders and the rest are day pupils. Girls make up approximately 30% of the intake. There are no day houses at Teddies and the 155 day pupils are expected to be in school from 8:30am – 9pm weekdays and 8:30am until late afternoon on a Saturday. There are seven boys and four girls' houses, each accommodating approximately 50-60 pupils. All the day pupils have a room within a boarding house and most have their own bed. This fairly unique feature ensures that there is no day versus boarding divide.

Although St Edward's is a distinguished and successful school its academic intake varies from the slightly above average to the outstandingly brilliant. Generally speaking, this is the ideal place for the less competitive types who would normally struggle in a more pressurized environment. However, the Oxbridge success rate at 10% is very commendable and clearly shows that there are plenty of pupils at Teddies with the intellectual capacity to win places at our top two universities. Those who go elsewhere tend to choose the usual suspects where public school educated students congregate in numbers such as Durham, Bristol, Exeter, Nottingham and St Andrews. Clearly, this is not a school for slackers. On a less positive note, A-Level results are not as impressive as some parents would wish for. The 2011 Financial Times League Tables which concentrates on the harder A-Level subjects, the ones recognized by Cambridge University, places St Edward's in the rather lowly position of 483. This compares unfavourably with Radley 23rd, Marlborough 76th and Wellington 220th but Teddies did perform better than Stowe ranked 529 and Bloxham at 656. However, things look better on the I.B. front. In 2010, the first set of I.B. results for the school ranked Teddies one of the top co-ed schools in the country according to the Times I.B. League Tables. The 2011 cohort did even better achieving a diploma average of just over 37 points (out of 45) placing Teddies in the top 10 of the Times I.B. table. One of the reasons why A level results appear relatively weaker is partly due to the fact that brighter students at Teddies tend to favour the I.B.

As one would expect from a school located in the genteel leafy suburbs of Oxford, the great majority of parents whose children attend this school are relatively well off middle class professionals or "City types". Boarding fees are staggeringly high at £28,700 and day fees surprisingly steep at £22,900. However, the usual scholarships and means tested bursaries exist which can help to reduce the financial burden. Teddies may be perceived by some as "less grand" than nearby Radley or Stowe but, it is certainly no less expensive! By the way, it is interesting to hear the views of some of the parents who have opted for Teddies instead of one of the other local public schools. Stowe it seems "has too many country types" whilst Radley is "ultra confident and highly competitive". These of course, are parental perceptions which may or may not be based on fact! Furthermore, Teddies parents are also keen to point out that both Radley and Stowe are located in "splendid isolation" whilst students at St Edward's can step out of the school gates into Summertown, visit the shops, make use of the local amenities and thus keep in touch with the outside world.

St Edward's is a flourishing and dynamic school with a reputation for being friendly and unpretentious. Pupils are drawn from over sixty prep schools with a significant number coming from the Dragon school a few streets away but, interestingly, not from Summer Fields which is also located in Summertown. The latter, a full boarding boys only prep school, is a main feeder for Eton, Radley, Harrow and Winchester and possibly attracts parents who prefer single sex full boarding schools. The Dragon on the other hand, as a co-ed school with a sizeable number of day pupils is where the academic and professional class from Oxford and its University prefer to send their children. In due course these bright pupils will transfer to Teddies, where many will achieve stellar results before moving on to Oxbridge.

The pastoral care at this school is second to none and according to some parents there is a great deal of support and mentoring. Unlike some senior schools which reputedly pay little more than lip service to these issues, Teddies takes pastoral duties very seriously. Moreover, the school also seems to have struck a reasonable balance on the important subjects of authority and discipline. Good behaviour and respect for others is actively encouraged and as an Anglican school, services are held two or three times a week in the charming chapel. One evening a week pupils are able to pop into the Chaplain's house for the delightfully named "More Tea Vicar" sessions, which provide an opportunity for the boys and girls to discuss absolutely anything including spiritual needs.

St Edward's enjoys a well deserved reputation as a strong sporting school and the main sports are rugby, rowing, cricket, hockey and tennis. A book about sport at this school "*Come on Teddy*" has recently been published. Rugby is very strong and well established and 15 pitches are available to accommodate a number of teams. The 1st XV as recently as 2007 only lost one game, reflecting the strength and depth of Teddies commitment to this sport and competitive needle games with neighbouring Radley always attract a great deal of interest. Rowing is another major sport which Teddies excels at and the school has its own boathouse. Every year St Edward's qualifies for the Princess Elizabeth Challenge Cup at Henley Royal Regatta and although the school has not lifted this trophy since 1999, Teddies rowing crews are always highly respected by rivals and usually perform admirably. Furthermore, the school has its own golf course, indoor pool, clay-pigeon shooting and an indoor rifle range. Sailing, netball and hockey complete the line up along with a huge number of other activities. Interestingly but perhaps not surprisingly, Polo is also played at Teddies and steadily growing in popularity. The fact that this rather exclusive sport is played at a school whose reputation is based on being "unpretentious and down to earth" reflects the changing nature of St Edward's catchment area.

Former pupils of St Edward's are generally referred to as OSE and a significant number have gone on to serve in the Armed Forces, in particular the Royal Air Force. Like many other public schools with a strong military tradition, the World Wars of the twentieth century have left their mark on the school. War heroes such as Group Captain Sir Douglas Bader (Reach for the Sky), Arthur Banks (George Cross), and Guy Gibson (Victoria Cross) are all products of this school. Other notable OSE include the author Kenneth Grahame, England rugby international James Forrester, Cheltenham Gold Cup winning jockey Sam Waley-Cohen, Channel 4 newscaster Jon Snow and Lord (Laurence) Olivier the actor and director. This list is by no means exhaustive as there are many other famous names that could be included. The few that I have chosen is mainly designed to reflect the diversity of talents that have emerged from this successful school.

It is perhaps worth remembering that the school's first Warden (Headmaster) Algernon Barrington Simeon, wanted St Edward's to produce "priests at home and abroad, lawyers, engineers, doctors, officers in the army and navy....the frankness and uprightness of whose dealings shows that they have a more sure end than money-making, and that they honour friendship as the highest gain in this life". These days of course, we live in a very different world and public school products in general seem to prefer the highly paid financial jobs in the City rather than become priests, soldiers, or engineers. Medicine and Law are still relatively popular but, far less than they were before "Big Bang" deregulated the City of London in 1986 and mega salaries in the square mile became the norm.

Parents looking for a co-educational school in the South East of England should most certainly consider St Edward's. The school is a wonderful blend of traditional values mixed with contemporary views and for a mixed ability educational establishment it achieves very respectable academic results. The "value added" factor at Teddies is one of the highest amongst public schools and consequently many pupils achieve better examination results than predicted. Sport, drama, music and many extra-curricular activities are excellently catered for and the overriding emphasis is to deliver a rounded and fulfilling education.

A LOVELY school!

"Now look carefully for any signs of prissiness" was the maternal word of advice when parking the car on our inaugural visit to St Mary's School in Ascot. Just then, as we rounded a corner, a large group of girls in climbing boots and outward bound gear, carrying heavy rucksacks "yomped" past ready to board a bus to their D of E activities. A meaningful look later, we were ready to be introduced to the school we would later select for our daughter.

The headmistress, Mrs Mary Breen, unequivocally sets the character of the school. In her words, everything about the school and its girls is "lovely" but this is a front for a steely determination to succeed and excel. And this school excels; it is a premier league school that concentrates on academic success but still delivers grounded and rounded, but invariably exceptional young women into society. Mrs Breen has a clear focus for the school and every aspect of the school is managed along her five core principles: The school is small, only 380 pupils; it is Roman Catholic so pupils need to be catholic; the very few who are not must take part in the catholic spirit of the school; it is a full boarding school with only a dozen or so day girls; it is rigorously academic but not to the exclusion of other activities including sports, music, arts and drama. Finally, it is a girls' school. This may seem a truism but at St Mary's it has significant meaning. Girls are encouraged to reach their full academic and personal potential undistracted by the lure of boys. Subjects can be chosen freely without the prejudice that pervades some mixed schools. Physics is for boys, history of art for girls, none of that here.

"Women in time to come will do much" is a quote often seen around St Mary's School and even today the words of a 17th century "heretic and rebel", convicted and imprisoned by the Inquisition, hold true. *Imprisoned in the same year as Galileo,* Mary Ward and the "English Ladies", her companions, had formed the Congregation of Jesus with whom she strove to educate women in and for society, not apart from it. This religious order established the school in 1885 and although no longer a convent school many of Mary Ward's foresighted principles apply in modern times and are actively pursued in St Mary's today.

St Mary's School stands in its own grounds in a sub-urban setting on the outskirts of Ascot, within easy reach of both the M3 and M4. Surrounded by gardens and sports grounds the buildings are more functional than impressive but once inside there is a homely feel to the place. The school has none of the feel of a convent with the significant exception in the spectacular chapel which sits central to the school and is the venue for assembly, religious but also musical gatherings. The school boasts a full-size, modern theatre where productions are put on continually as part of the arts curriculum. The arts studio is equally well equipped and the work produced by pupils in some cases quite breath-taking. The swimming pool, tennis courts, AstroTurf and field games pitches are also evidence that this school is so much more than an academic hothouse.

Although a stated aim of Mrs Breen's to be small, the school's size is limited by the available boarding places. The school takes in girls aged 11 and 13 drawing its population from a wide range of feeder schools (rarely more than 2 or 3 from the same school) but certainly from an eclectic international set with a smattering of royalty thrown in. Each year the school accepts some 40 girls at age 11 who need to go through a rigorous selection with exams, group activity and interviews. Many apply, relatively few are accepted. A further 20 go through a similar process for entry at age 13. An active programme of integration ensures that the late joiners are integrated into the existing group very quickly. The unorthodox house system helps. Girls are accommodated together by year group with dormitories no larger than 4 beds. The boarding is managed by a team of residential boarding staff. Quite separate from the accommodation is the house system that applies to sports and social activity with girls mixed across the year groups. Each house is managed by academic staff, often a couple who live on site. Girls are allocated to these houses by the Headmistress without parental input. Indicative of this school's ethos, very few girls leave before finishing hence very few places come available later on. For their final year 6th-formers move into the Mary Ward complex. With rooms grouped around a court yard, the girls have the opportunity to prepare for life at university. They have individual study/bedrooms with communal sitting rooms and kitchens as found on a university campus. The girls can cook independently and have access to their own laundry facilities. As the girls progress to the senior years they also become more engaged in the running of the school and well-defined but very low key peer discipline is practiced with a head girl and the customary prefect system in place. Almost all pupils go on to red brick universities, with Edinburgh, Bristol, Durham and Exeter being popular, and a strong proportion go on to Oxford and Cambridge; indeed in the current Upper Sixth, 12 out of a total of 60 girls already have offers from Oxford or Cambridge, and more will apply post A level. A few girls each year go to Ivy League American Universities.

So why St Mary's for us? We had not considered a girls' school for our daughter but on the recommendation from her headmaster and having googled this school's outstanding record, we visited. We were

201

smitten by St Mary's the moment we set foot in the place, met the staff and saw the grace and easy confidence of the pupils here. We saw how girls could be vigorous, enthusiastic and unselfconscious in their own company and experienced the vast range of activities that these girls engaged in; the music is outstanding, the art exceptional, the academic record impressive. We were convinced by the girls' freedom to choose their own subjects rather than those deemed suitable for girls. Only in our first year at the school, we have seen how this school has made its mark already. We are quite sure that, like so many before her, our daughter in time will come to do much.

The author John Bleeker is a wing commander in the Royal Air Force who with his wife Susie, a National Health Service hospital director, lives in the Test Valley in Hampshire. They have a son at the excellent Canford School and, thinking specifically academic single-sex education more suited to their daughter, sent her to St Mary's School in Ascot.

ST PAUL'S SCHOOL

Lonsdale Road

London SW13 9JT

www.stpaulsschool.org.uk

0208 748 9162

FOUNDED in 1509 by John Colet the Dean of St Paul's Cathedral the school moved to its current site in Barnes, North London in 1968. The buildings are typical of this period and therefore quite different to the image one has of the quintessential English public school. However the activities, lessons and calibre of teaching place St Paul's into the highest echelons of private education.

Last year St Paul's was placed third in the Financial Times league table, it is often in pole position and last year sent a staggering 41% of its boys to Oxford or Cambridge. Other popular destinations are Bristol, Warwick, Durham, UCL, Imperial and Edinburgh. Of the 180 or so leavers between 20 and 25 head for Yale, Princeton or Harvard every year. 98.3% of boys achieved A* B grades at A-Level and of those 89% were A* As. These figures are available only from the school or their website as they have withdrawn from submitting their results to public league tables. This is a trend being followed by many public schools which would prefer their schools to be considered on more than just academic statistics. However there is no getting away from the fact that this is a very academic school for very bright boys. St Paul's leaves other boys only, largely day schools in the shade with Tonbridge its nearest competitor being ranked 9th and Merchant Taylors lagging somewhat further behind at 35 on this league table. The only true rival to which St Paul's can be compared is

Westminster (although they do have girls in the Sixth Form) which is placed 1ˢᵗ and sends 48% to Oxbridge. Around half of all boys join the school aged 13 from their own feeder prep, Colet Court. The remaining boys come from prep schools around London. Registration for entry at 13+ opens in May four years before starting and is open only until the following May. Following a report from the prep school head candidates will be invited for a short 20 minute interview which is very informal. An offer will be made within ten days but is conditional on achieving the required marks in the Common Entrance Examination or Scholarship exam. The previous High Master, Dr George Stephen made huge strides in the effort to make St Paul's truly needs blind. If you meet the means tested bursary criteria ad have a son who would be up to the academic rigours of such an education then you would be very well advised to apply for a place. Of the 850 pupils only about 30 board but the boarding house is run with the same efficiency that you would expect to find at a full boarding school. The tutor system at St Paul's carries on this pastoral care. Each tutor is responsible for around three boys per year group, meeting with boys daily as well as being a regular point of contact with parents. As the boys stay with the same tutor throughout their five years at St Paul's a very strong relationship is often formed, important when one considers the advice and influence that the tutor has in the latter stages of senior school when university options are discussed and followed through at great length.

Although day schools are often not considered as being particularly strong on sport or extra-curricular activities that isn't the case here. With 45 acres of playing fields surrounding the school and direct frontage onto the River Thames rowing is popular and results have been excellent. They have won the Princess Elizabeth Challenge Cup at Henley four times, although last year were beaten by St Andrews School who hail from Delaware in the United States. Rugby is also competitively played as are Fives. The school can boast its own Fencing Salle, a 25 meter indoor pool, games hall and 10 tennis courts. More importantly though is the way in which boys are encouraged to take part in physical activities. There is the weekly "games half" devoting an entire afternoon to sport, timetabled PE lessons as well as the use of the 100 minute lunch break which is often used by most boys to get involved with anything from football to ultimate Frisbee.

With a school of this calibre the slew of Old Pauline's reads like an edition of Who's Who. Notable though are the diarist Samuel Pepys, poet John Milton, historian and television programme maker Dan Snow, Editor of The Times James Harding, eminent biologist Professor Robert Winston and the current Chancellor of the Exchequer George Osborne.

Schools generally like to say that they don't have a "type" of child that they turn out and perhaps reviewing this list you may think that to be true but St Pauls is definitely a school only for the very cleverest of boys.

Brook Green

Hammersmith W6 7BS

www.spgs.org

0207 603 2288

WHEN St Paul's School for Boys was founded in 1509 John Colet's mission was to "educate children of all nations and countries". It was, however, only in 1904 when the St Paul's Foundation decided that girls should also benefit from this noble intention that St Paul's Girl's School was established in Hammersmith. With 700 girls hailing from 24 countries this aim finally seems to have been achieved.

The current Headmistress is Clarissa Farr, an intellectual and political trend setter. Her vision for the future of education and importantly how children translate their educational opportunities into a very fast changing workplace are often commented on following her articles published in national newspapers. With superb top down leadership the environment at SPGS is liberal and informal perhaps aided by the lack of uniform, girls may wear whatever they choose within the bounds of decorum and neat jeans, t-shirts and sweaters tend to prevail. It certainly encourages individuality and flair in these young ladies. This relaxed and friendly environment ensures that pupils feel very well looked after. Under the sister scheme each new Year 7 girl is paired up with a Year 10 or 11 pupil who will see her through the first weeks or months meeting regularly to guide them through the adjustment to senior school.

Entry into the school is at age 11 with only a very few Sixth Form places being available. You will need to register a year prior to your daughter's potential admission. In November she will be called to take a computer test, very cleverly designed to weed out those who have been tutored or coached and indeed the school is very particular that if you have followed this route that it be declared. With a report from the prep school head girls are shortlisted for an interview and tests in Maths, English and Comprehension in January. By February the decisions have been made and offers sent out. On reviewing the outstanding academic results at St Pauls it is obvious that entry is very competitive. The school ranked 6th on the Financial Times League table and sent an absolutely astonishing 52% of girls to Oxford or Cambridge in 2011. 48.4% of girls achieved much coveted A* grades at A Level and in all 93.2% of girls could boast A* As. By Year 12 each girl will have her own academic mentor, a relationship which is very beneficial in the next steps decision making process. In fact it is very interesting to look at the table of leavers destinations, not only are they the top British universities, other than Oxford and Cambridge, Imperial, UCL and Bristol feature highly, there are also a number of girls who choose the American Ivy Leagues to further their education. The degree courses are very wide ranging, art, music, languages, the sciences, medicine and mathematics all being listed. This variety plays itself out in the distinguished list of Old Paulinas; journalists Sophie Raworth and Rachel Johnson to former Deputy Prime Minister Harriet Harman as well as a smattering of much lauded actresses, Rachel Weisz, Imogen Stubbs, Emily Mortimer and the late Natasha Richardson.

However it's not all work and no play. There are over a hundred clubs and 28 sporting activities on offer. The usual netball and tennis are popular and the school has a fairly new sports hall which can even accommodate indoor lacrosse. There is badminton, trampolining, a dance studio and large 25m pool for swimming, diving, water polo as well as scuba diving.

For a day school fees are quite steep at an average of £6500 per term but there is a target to fund up to 20% of girls through a means tested bursary. There are a few scholarships available with an award of around £250 and in the case of music scholarships free tuition in the chosen instrument. The Nora Day Music Scholarship which is means tested may offer a 50% remission in fees as well as free tuition in two instruments.

Being situated in West London girls at this school are very savvy and cosmopolitan, a perfect reflection of life in our capital city. Paulinas are generally able to travel to school by bus or tube and navigate their way through the hustle and bustle of London life. Their social lives revolve around art galleries, theatre and concerts and the vast majority of girls are from intellectual and creative families. It has been said before that St Pauls Girls is an outstanding school but worth saying again that the raw material is exceptional.

Mario di Monaco with Kerry Rhodes

STOWE SCHOOL

Stowe

Buckingham MK18 5EH

www.stowe.org.uk

01280 818323

FOR an educational institution which only came into existence in 1923 Stowe has done remarkably well in establishing itself as one of the great English public schools. Set in 750 acres of beautiful parkland, much of it designed by Capability Brown, many of the buildings and park are open to the public through the National Trust. The original Stowe House, an elegant Palladian building of exquisite beauty remains the piece de resistance of this famous school. Many believe that Stowe is one of the most attractive schools in the land thanks to the creative brilliance of Vanbrugh, Adam and Kent who have all played a part in creating this splendid haven in the heart of Buckinghamshire.

Stowe is a rather grand country school whose pupils come from all over the U.K. Here you will find the offspring of the landed gentry of Northumberland, North Yorkshire or Norfolk rubbing shoulders with the sons and daughters of successful professionals from the South East. However, the image of Stowe as a suitable repository for the rich but not so bright applies less now than was once the case even though the school still accommodates a fair number of boys whose fathers were educated at Eton. Under the brilliant leadership of its present Headmaster, the charming and erudite Dr Anthony Wallersteiner, the school is moving in a different trajectory. For starters the academic bar has been raised and an increasing number of clever pupils are looking to Stowe as their first choice. All prospective pupils will need to obtain a minimum of 50% at Common Entrance to win a place. Not surprisingly A Level results have improved substantially and the A Level A/B pass rate now stands at a respectable 76%. Moreover, six or seven pupils per year win places at Oxbridge and most other Stoics end up at "Rah" universities such as Newcastle, Bristol, Exeter or Oxford Brooks. Naturally, this place is never going to compete with academic institutions such as Westminster, Winchester or Eton. However, the Headmaster is keen to ensure that in future Stowe does not lose out to the likes of Radley, Rugby, Oundle or Uppingham. In fact he appears to be spectacularly gaining rather than losing as the number of pupils at Stowe has risen in the last four years from 640 to 790 with 90% being full boarders. Remarkably, this has been achieved at a time when fewer pupils are enrolling at private schools.

For a place whose reputation has been anything other than academic, Stowe has produced a disproportionately large number of very successful people who have made major contributions in fields as diverse as the arts, the armed forces, law, medicine, commerce and politics. Apparently, a recent survey looking at the published obituaries in our quality newspapers revealed that Stowe was the third most commonly quoted school. Clearly, the Alma Mater of Richard Branson, Lord Sainsbury, Earl Haig and the late Prince Rainier of Monaco to mention but a few, has played a major role in educating the Nation's Great and Good. Interestingly, but perhaps not surprisingly, Stowe has produced more Masters of Fox Hounds than any other school in the country and still has a pack of Beagles. However, with the hunting ban still in place chasing a live hare is not a legal option. Furthermore, as one would expect from a country school with a fair number of rural pupils, shooting in its various forms, remains popular with significant numbers of boys and girls taking part and competing very successfully. Polo is also popular at Stowe and the school has had some notable success in this rather exclusive sport.

Like many other boys boarding schools Stowe has had to adapt to modern trends in order to survive and thrive. Having initially only admitted girls in the Sixth Form the school has recently become fully co-educational and the aim is achieve a ratio of 60% boys and 40% girls. Moreover, some 10% of the intake is now made up of day pupils. This number is unlikely to increase as most people who look to Stowe are attracted to its rural location and boarding ethos. There are of course some dyed in the wool traditionalists who lament the passing of an era and wish that Stowe had remained a single sex educational establishment. Had this been the case, the school, would in all probability have struggled to make ends meet. However, the arrival of girls has done more than just fill empty places. Many believe that they have added an exciting new dimension to the place and have most definitely raised academic standards. Stowe girls are often thought of as being attractive Sloaney types who are intelligent but also love a good party!

212

Parents frequently ask what sort of pupils would thrive at Stowe and what makes this school different from many others like it? Clearly, if this school is of interest to you a visit is mandatory and a chat with the Headmaster highly recommended. Also, make certain that you quiz some of the pupils and parents if possible. My personal view is that the individual who is likely to flourish at Stowe is one who is blessed with a multitude of talents but not obsessed with academic success or getting into Oxbridge. The school likes to focus on the bigger picture and whether its rugby, music, art or shooting your offspring is keen on, rest assured that Stowe will cater to a high standard and allow your son or daughter to achieve his or her full potential. Those with artistic talents are particularly well served. The shear visual beauty of this place generates a strong inspirational force which few other schools can match. Not surprisingly, the art department is extremely strong and an array of impressive artistic pieces was on display throughout the buildings when we visited the school in the spring of 2011.

Music is also held in high esteem and talented musicians are revered at Stowe. The vast majority of pupils play at least one instrument and many two or more. In 2011 a boy from our sons prep school, Lockers Park in Hertfordshire, won a music scholarship to Stowe by exhibiting extraordinary talents on the drums, the saxophone, guitar and piano. Famous musical Stoics have included George Melly – Jazz Singer, Anthony Negus – Conductor of the Welsh Opera and Roger Hodgson – founder of the hugely successful group Supertramp whose most famous album Breakfast in America was a major hit when I was at university some thirty years ago!

As one would expect from a fashionable school charging fees in excess of £28000 per annum sporting facilities are outstanding. The school excels at rugby, polo, cricket, lacrosse and shooting. Last year Stowe reached the semi-final of the Daily Mail Rugby Cup and the polo team is one of the best amongst the exclusive public schools that actually play this game. The enviable cricket pitch provides spectacular views of both the school's main buildings and the surrounding countryside. The facilities are such that the Northamptonshire County Cricket team play their matches here. Needless to say cricket is played with passion at this school and the addition of ex-England cricketer Darren Gough to the coaching staff is likely to make Stowe an even more formidable opponent. Girls Lacrosse is equally successful with an excellent showing at this year's Midlands Tournament, taking home the trophy for the first time

As mentioned earlier, Stowe is the perfect place for the academically competent all-rounder who is prepared to accept that whilst this school will allow them to develop into confident and articulate teenagers, it may not necessarily provide a gateway to Oxbridge. Moreover, if your heart is set on medicine at University College London, economics at the LSE or engineering at Imperial College this will require some serious book work and a large dose of good fortune. Naturally, some Stoics do make it to our most prestigious colleges and from there into glittering careers. However, as things stand at present, most Stoics seem to end up at desirable but less academic Russell Group universities. The army, which has always had more than its fair share of Stoics, still remains a popular choice and the world of property, especially those who deal in expensive country houses also remains an attractive destination. Once upon a time the City also recruited a substantial number from this school. However, "Big Bang" in 1986 deregulated the financial markets and paved the way for foreign banks to set up shop and flourish in London. Since then Stoics have become less prevalent within the Square Mile, as American banks in particular, seem to prefer academic high flyers capable of generating huge sums of money rather than someone who has simply attended the "right" school.

Modern day Stowe is an exciting and lively school where pupils enjoy a first class education in a serene and inspirational environment. The boys and girls who attend this school are on the whole polite and well aware that their world is a rarefied and privileged one which only a fortunate few can access. Most Stoics whom I have had the good fortune to meet along the salmon rivers or shooting fields, have come across as confident characters with impeccable manners and impressive social skills. That said,

I have also met people who find the plumy voices associated with Stoics patronising and irritating. However, this is hardly surprising in a country like ours where as George Bernard Shaw astutely wrote in Pygmalion, "an Englishman has to only open his mouth to be despised by another Englishman!"

In summary, a traditional public school set in wonderful surroundings. Under the guidance of its charming and highly intelligent Headmaster Anthony Wallersteiner, the school's popularity is rapidly heading north. Academic results are fast improving and the school is steaming ahead. Stoics it seems can once again stroll along the Kings Road or Kensington High Street with their heads held high!

TONBRIDGE

Tonbridge

Kent TN9 1JP

www.tonbridge-school.co.uk

01732 365555

TONBRIDGE School was founded in 1553 by Sir Andrew Judde under Letters Patent of King Edward VI. Sited on 150 acres in the centre of Tonbridge almost 100 acres are devoted to playing fields and various sporting activities. There are 763 boys in the school, aged 13-18, of whom 439 are boarders occupying seven boarding houses, and 324 day boys who are divided amongst five houses. The school is single sex and apparently there are no plans to admit girls. Week day uniform consists of the traditional school blazer, white shirt, school trousers, grey socks and black plain shoes. Despite the large number of day boys Tonbridge is run very much along the lines of a full boarding school.

Although Tonbridge enjoys a national reputation for its strong academic and sporting achievements, the school does not always receive the credit it justly deserves. Why for example, do English parents who reside beyond the South East happily send their sons to Radley, Eton or Harrow but only occasionally to Tonbridge? Some have suggested that this is simply because Tonbridge has a large number of day boys and this tends to deter the landed types from the shires who often prefer full boarding establishments. Moreover, Tonbridge is on the whole fairly unpretentious and people who see themselves as socially superior would not necessarily flock to this school. Interestingly, a school master at Tonbridge who was educated at Radley, told me that he found it odd that some of his pupils often referred to his old school as "posh". Girls from nearby Benenden (Princess Anne's old school), are most definitely a "posh" lot; but it is no secret that many wish for an Etonian boyfriend more than any other. Rather depressingly, within the rarefied world of our major public schools, social class still seems to be an important issue.

Whether or not Tonbridge is considered a socially fashionable school is largely immaterial. Prospective parents should pay far more attention to the fact that this educational establishment is widely regarded as a solid "first division" public school with an outstanding academic record. According to the highly respected Financial Times A-Level performance table, which focuses mainly on the harder subjects, in 2011 Tonbridge was ranked spectacularly high at number 9. This compares with Winchester 7th, Eton 13th, Radley 23rd, Harrow 39th, Charterhouse 84th, Marlborough 76th and Wellington College 220th. Clearly, this place is among the top performing boarding schools in the country and unsurprisingly most of the pupils gain places at some of our most prestigious universities with approximately 20% going to Oxford or Cambridge. A significant number end up at Imperial College, University College London, Durham, Nottingham and Bristol. Bearing in mind that this is a mixed ability school these impressive achievements seem to imply that this is not a place for slackers. Hard work coupled with excellent teaching is what one can expect at Tonbridge. However, one must appreciate that all of this will not come cheaply. Annual boarding fees at Tonbridge will set you back an eye watering £31,000 making this school marginally more expensive than the Eton, Harrow or Winchester.

Entry to Tonbridge is competitive but not horrendously difficult. Three years before entry at 13+ the school will conduct an interview and computer based test as well as requesting a confidential report from the head of your son's current school. Three months later conditional offers will be made although parents are only required to accept or decline the offer 18 months prior to entry. To guarantee the place 60% is required in the Common Entrance Examination. I suspect that the academic entry bar has been set at this modest level to ensure that boys whose talents lie in other areas such as sport, music or drama are still attracted to the school. Forty five scholarships are offered each year, 22 of which are awarded for academic achievement. The remission in fees for these scholarships is in the range of 10%-50% which by modern standards is quite generous. Additionally in a typical year there are 10 or more music scholarships, 8 art, drama or technology scholarships and 3 Cowdrey (sports) scholarships.

The excellent reputation of this school together with its close proximity to London and its airports has not escaped the attention of the international community who wish to educate their sons privately in Britain. Chinese and other overseas boys are now fairly prevalent at Tonbridge and their work ethos is such that many eventually progress to either Oxbridge or the top London Colleges such as U.C.L. Personally, I admire and applaud schools that have made efforts to attract pupils from beyond our shores. To survive and prosper in a global economy, we need to ensure that our offspring learn to interact with people from different cultures. After all, the civilized world does not end at the white cliffs of Dover. Thankfully, although Tonbridge is located in Kent, the so called "garden of England", this place is most definitely not a parochial school for "Little Englanders".

There is a strong sporting tradition at Tonbridge and the school excels at rugby, cricket and football. Rugby is played to a phenomenal high standard and not so long ago the school achieved a remarkable record by remaining unbeaten for three consecutive years. One wonders how many other major public schools have remained undefeated for two years let alone three. Nowadays, most rugby playing schools such as Radley or Harrow would be delighted if they went through one season without losing a match. As for cricket it is hardly surprising to learn that the school attended by the legendary cricketer Sir Colin Cowdrey, takes this game very seriously. Sir Colin cricketing career lasted from 1950 to 1976 and he was the first cricketer to play in 100 test matches for England. His formidable skills with the bat were a joy to watch and by the end of his international career he had accumulated 22 test centuries.

Tonbridge is one of our leading independent senior schools and under the leadership of Tim Haynes, the present Headmaster, the reputation of this educational establishment has been rapidly heading north. This place is now up there with the very best and those boys fortunate enough to attend this school can confidently look forward to a thrilling and successful future.

One such boy is James Estlin who left Tonbridge in 2011 and is off to read Economics at Durham University. This is what he has to say about his old school:

James Estlin, Tonbridge School 2006 – 2011

Though predominantly a boarding establishment, Tonbridge School has also sought to educate day boys ever since its foundation in 1553. The School currently consists of seven boarding houses and five day houses, and operates a 60:40 boarding today boy ratio. I attended Tonbridge School as a day boy of Welldon House between 2006-2011.

There are several reasons why one might opt for a day education at Tonbridge. Being a day boy offers greater independence and privacy, as well as the ability to withdraw from the (often fairly intense) school environment each evening. Past notions of prejudice against day boys no longer exist at the School, and sport, drama, music and all other pursuits are just as open today boys as they are to boarders.

Regardless of whether you choose a day or a boarding education at Tonbridge, the School will provide you with a well-rounded and first-rate education. Tonbridge's academic pedigree is evident in its high Oxbridge success rate, and consistently strong exam results. Sport, too, is extremely competitive, with the School's rugby and cricket clubs occupying particularly prominent positions on the public schools circuit. The School runs a popular and highly-regarded Combined Cadet Force (which in 2010 celebrated its 150th anniversary) and music and drama are also performed to a high standard within the School.

Every pupil at Tonbridge is strongly encouraged to participate in any co-curricular activity that they are interested in pursuing, regardless of past experience or ability. There are timetabled slots dedicated purely to such endeavours three afternoons a week. This all-inclusive attitude is just as prevalent on the sports pitches. The rugby club consistently fields up to 22 teams, ensuring that anyone who wants to play Tonbridge rugby is able to do so.

Tonbridge is an elite institution, but it is not elitist and it eagerly encourages participation regardless of ability. It is the absolute commitment to this ethos which I truly believe defines the School. Perhaps it even sets Tonbridge apart.

TUDOR HALL SCHOOL

Wykham Park

Oxfordshire OX16 9UR

www.tudorhallschool.com

01295 263434

Heather Morley

"Aesthetics: do they matter in a school? Discuss."

I FELT like I was back in an A-level discussion class when I visited Tudor Hall on a cold, crisp and brilliant January afternoon. Having attended the world's least attractive school (1960's building blocks in primary colours) my heart sinks whenever I recall my days there, in spite of lovely friends, some excellent teaching and it forming a successful springboard for university and beyond. The only source of my antipathy, I have since reasoned, is the cumulative effect of years spent in such ugly surroundings. If this theory holds true, then the alumnae of Tudor Hall must be blissfully happy till the end of their days.

Set in elegant parkland, itself surrounded by well-stewarded farming acres, Tudor Hall's stunning principal building is a wonderfully English hybrid – in parts a Jacobean, Georgian and Victorian mansion. Whatever has been built since has been added sympathetically, carved out of the glowing creamy Cotswold stone that forms dry stone walls and picture-perfect cottages in this part of Oxfordshire. As you enter the grand front door, you are met by a huge basket of logs which feeds the generous fire in the entrance hall. Whilst waiting to see the headmistress, I was offered tea and home-made biscuits. An off-duty teacher walked past with his dog, no doubt having had a pleasant stroll through the grounds. I felt like I was in heaven!

My admiration for the place, however, goes well beyond the cosy and welcoming atmosphere. This is a school that has quietly revolutionised itself in the last few years. A recent Financial Times article noted that, despite not having provided the world with a vast number of captains of industry, Tudor Hall had managed to improve its results and rise up A-level league tables faster than any other school. About 80-85% of girls achieve grades A*-B at A-level, very respectable. That's what our excellent local grammar school achieves. One current parent says: "Tudor is as academic as a child can be. The girls are pushed hard but not over the top – it is very capable of taking the brightest to the very highest level." It sends around 5% (2-3 girls) a year to Oxbridge, the majority of others gaining places at Leeds, Newcastle, Durham, Bristol, Exeter as well as Art Foundation colleges. No doubt the school spawns some scientists too – I previously visited the school on Open Day and the Chemistry teacher enthralled us with various methods to make explosions.

How has the school evolved? Surely the catalyst has been its feisty Welsh Headmistress, Wendy Griffiths. After reading for a Biology degree, she completed a PGCE and became fascinated by the positive effect that teaching could have on children. She progressed from a Portsmouth comprehensive, through Tormead School, Guildford and St Catherine's, Bramley then arrived at Tudor Hall in 2oo4. She has vision, commitment, obvious intelligence and enormous energy – and has increased numbers from 270 girls when she arrived to 330 in the school today ("won't increase beyond that"). Wendy Griffiths is to what Tudor Hall used to be (finishing school for the not-so-bright) what balsamic vinegar is to olive oil. The combination of the traditional, wholesome, wholeheartedly nice school with the ultra-dynamic Miss Griffiths is very exciting. She has modernised facilities, brought in professional working practices, vastly improved pastoral care and yet had the sense to maintain its caring family atmosphere. And she hasn't finished yet.

She must be popular too. As I munched my way through my pre-interview snack, a charming recent alumna popped in to see everyone. This apparently happens frequently. In a few weeks' time, Miss Griffiths and her senior team are travelling by minibus to Newcastle in order to spend a few hours catching up with Old Tudorians now ensconced at university in that city and nearby Durham. Next term they will so the same in Leeds and the following one they will journey to Bristol. Which other schools would have such dedicated staff that would devote their night off to such a purpose? And can you imagine many schools where old girls would wish to spend a Saturday night in the company of their ex-teachers? They talk a lot here about focus on the individual, and the importance of relationships between pupils, staff and families. I can see that they mean what they say.

A current parent says "we chose Tudor because we wanted a small all-girls school … for her to have the chance to be a big fish in a small pond". Certainly the two upper sixth formers I met seemed to think they'd benefited. In both cases they had close relatives who had attended the school. They identified that good friendships for life were the most important thing they'd gained from their time there. They liked the facts of the school being small enough to know everyone, and of it being relaxed owing to the absence of boys – no need for makeup or jewellery, and no competition between girls on that score. From Year 11 most girls are excused from wearing school uniform which means that they are to be found in jeans and sweatshirts. "Happy" and "friendly" were two words that cropped up a lot in their language. This is compounded in the view of the deputy head of a leading feeder prep: "Tudor Hall takes a broad range of girls and does well by them all. They seem to leave very grounded – not at all arrogant or conceited."

What do they get up to at weekends? Contrary to some reports that Tudor girls are to be found roaming around Banbury and Oxford every weekend, this is only an infrequent excursion. Far more likely they will be engaging in their "super-curricular" programme – timetabled Dance, Sport or Prep on a Saturday morning, followed by a creative or philosophical project in the afternoon (the 12 year-olds I met had recently designed posters about the Amanda Knox court case). Sundays usually feature Chapel in the morning and a major activity or sometimes a Social with a boys' school. One parent opines that Socials are too infrequent. When they do happen it seems mostly to be Radley that features. Or perhaps it is just that the Radleians are more memorable than the others! That said, the younger girls I met were about to join Summer Fields for a drama workshop and the school states that there is an ongoing programme of other joint events – maths workshops, science days, various lectures, etc. Parents can expect to take their girls home every three weeks or so for the weekend, but are welcome at matches in between. Girls are permitted to phone home for up to an hour every weekday evening from the Twos (Year 8) and up, which seems very relaxed compared with some other schools. Not that most use up their time allowance – they are far too busy with activities.

What does the school look for in girls who apply for places? Miss Griffiths cites a list of attributes such as sparky, talented (in various assorted ways), enthusiastic, passionate (about almost anything). They look for a broad mix and there is something appealing in the girls whom she says "will be a handful". She also gives places regularly to girls whom she thinks will get a lot out of the school. Bursaries are at a higher level now than ever before, and they are not necessarily awarded to the gifted and talented girls.

Tudor either suffers or benefits from the impression that it is a "smart" school. There are now, it seems "almost no" titled pupils here and little any more in the way of "old money" - will that disappoint the arrivistes?! Instead most parents seem to be professionals - doctors, lawyers, accountants, City types. They live in the shires (Oxfordshire, Gloucestershire, Northamptonshire) around the school. A few from Norfolk/Suffolk and a fair few from London. Not many foreign students, maybe less than 10% non-caucasians, unlike the better-known schools. That is more to do with lack of publicity abroad, there is no deliberate policy on the part of the school.

The big sports here are Lacrosse, Hockey, Netball and Tennis. There is a modern Astroturf pitch, an indoor sports hall and swimming pool. I have never seen more beautiful tennis courts (back to the point about Aesthetics again!) as they are contained within a charming old walled garden complete with architecturally perfect pavilion. Currently there is a national Under 17 high jump champion at the school, as well as a 15 year-old GB sailor who will be competing in the European Championships this summer. One current parent states that Sport has come on "hugely" this year. Certainly when you consider the development programme (see later) it is clear that the school means to add weight to its sporting profile.

I asked what might surprise me about the school. Despite not being a hothouse, it still managed to churn out Nicola Pease/Odey, city doyenne par excellence. In her illustrious company as old girls are: Julia Peyton-Jones, Director of the Serpentine Gallery; Sacha Bonsor, leading journalist; Candida Bond, sculptor; Katherine Hooker, tailor to the Duchess of Cambridge. In the latter case, I am not in the least surprised. Art, DT, Textiles seem to be already of an exceptional standard (the teachers I met were completely inspirational) and those areas will come in for significant improving expenditure over the next few years. Bravo! It seems to be a relief all round that there are no famous celebrities or "slebs" in the sorority. There is a very young staff, 60% being under 40 and 28% being under 30. This goes some way to explain the lack of stuffiness in the school. There is also a surprising amount that the girls do for others: the school motto being "*Habeo ut Dem*" – "I have that I may give". A group of 20 sixth formers will embark shortly on trips to Bolivia, India and South Africa to assist in aid projects. These are not brain floss girls intent on a lifetime of lunches and shopping.

What of the school's future? A ten million pound budget is earmarked to provide a new 80-seater Drama studio, improved Dance and Gymnastic space, new swimming pool, eight-room classroom block, improvements to boarding facilities and a café. That's within the next ten years, maybe five. Oh and they bought a feeder prep school not long ago. Phew!

So amidst the beautiful surroundings, the bucolic perfection, this is a gem of a school. I was trying to describe it to my daughter the first time I went there a couple of years ago. I said it was a bit like Malory Towers in that it would teach decency, good manners and that it would provide her with a team of friends for life. I would amend that now to say that it would also provide her with an excellent education and an ambition to reach for the stars. This school is a class act. Go and see it.

Andrew Crowston – an Old Oakhamiam

UPPINGHAM has a rich history being founded by Archdeacon Robert Johnson in 1584. His endowment and legacy was to found, a Grammar Schools and Almshouse in both Uppingham and in Oakham.

In both cases, the original Grammar School building still stands near the parish church showing the historical yet still strong links to the Anglican Church. At Oakham the Almshouse was demolished in the 19th century, whilst that of Uppingham was absorbed into the school during the 17th century. As in many other rural towns, the Grammar School at Uppingham remained a small local school, although the use of the former Almshouse building enabled it to take in boarders. One distinctive feature was the provision of individual studies for its boys by 1800. Uppingham remained a small town, one not served by its own rail connection until 1894.

Major change came in 1853, when 32-year-old Edward Thring was appointed Headmaster. Thring was born in Somerset and was sent to Eton and from there progressed to King's College, Cambridge, as a scholar, then a Fellow. Like many of his contemporaries, he went into the Church, firstly as a curate in Gloucester, where he also did some teaching

228

at the National School, and then in Berkshire, where he took in private pupils. Thring brought in major changes that set the core principles that define the character of the school.

To meet his educational philosophy, he advocated a much wider curriculum than that of Dr Arnold at Rugby – a narrow diet of classics, ancient history, mathematics and divinity. To this Thring added French, German, Chemistry, Art, Woodwork, Music (including visiting instrumentalists). In sport, the school appointed the first cricket professional as coach and had both the first purpose-built gymnasium and heated indoor swimming pool in any school. These developments put Uppingham as one of the pioneers of development and advancement at public schools during the Victorian period, policies copied widely by all other schools. This period plays an important period in defining and setting the foundation of Uppingham today.

By the time Thring died in office in 1887, Uppingham School had a national reputation. Thring was an original thinker and a man who could put theory into practice. He would have been very difficult to work with, but today we can see him as a man with a vision way ahead of his time.

Uppingham is a co-educational independent school with approximately 780 boys and girls, located in the picturesque market town of Uppingham, Rutland. Set in central rural England and a big attraction to those families not wanting the distraction of a large town whilst still less than 2 hours drive from London. The school has beautiful limestone buildings, impressive quads and 60+ acres of sporting grounds, amongst the largest in the country.

Uppingham counts as one of the top co-educational independent schools in the central Midlands belt that also includes local rivals Rugby, Oundle, Bedford School and Oakham School. Uppingham is virtually full boarding with 95 percent plus of all pupils boarding. 15 houses accommodate the boys and girls giving the school a strong collegiate atmosphere. The number of girls has grown over the last 20 years, and now account for 40 % of boarding pupils. The school retains its strong religious, Church of England history and has a beautiful chapel were attendance is compulsory 5 days a week still. This all makes Uppingham still popular amongst families from the south Midland counties, East Anglia and southern counties. 75% of parents come from professional families whilst 25% still come from wealthy families linked to agriculture.

Uppingham is not horrendously selective; the school does though require admission tests in maths and English, 30 minutes each, followed by an interview from a senior member of staff. Conditional places are then awarded requiring pupils to obtain typically 55% in common entrance. Academic results at GCSE and A level are strong given the less rigorous selection process. Like many schools Uppingham's A levels results have been improving steadily over the last ten years. In 2002 37% of pupils achieved A*/A whilst in 2011 63% achieved the top two A levels grades. The latest FT guide for independent schools placed Uppingham 86th. This puts Uppingham in a league similar to its rivals Oundle 74, Rugby 96, Oakham 147, Bedford School 112 whilst a step behind the more academically selective Perse School Cambridge 21st and Harrow 24th.

Uppingam's leavers gravitate to the top Universities and popular destinations include; Newcastle, Leeds, Oxford Brookes, Edinburgh, Bristol, Durham, and Nottingham. Oxbridge entrance is a credible 8-12% per annum with 16 boys and girls gaining Oxbridge entrance in 2011. Gap year is popular with up to 50% of pupils taking a GAP. The arts and humanities account for the majority, approximately 70% of degrees chosen whilst Science subjects account for approximately a third. With the new Science school due to open in 2012 this will surely only strengthen.

Three books tell Uppingham's story:

Uppingham by the Sea.

By God's Grace, by Bryan Matthews, 1984, History of the School.

A picture book of a unique school by Warwick Metcalfe, line drawings by a young art master at the school;

Eminent Uppinghamians, by Bryan Matthews, voted the worst book in 1986 and *Uppingham by the Sea* is published by a Loughborough firm who specialised in local reprints.

Accommodation at Uppingham now comprises 15 houses, which are dotted around the town and School estate. As boarders account typically for 95+ of the pupils at the school, the House and its collegiate atmosphere still play a important pastoral role. Nine Houses are for boys (ages 13–18), four for girls (ages 13–18) and two for sixth-form girls only. Houses are split into three geographic areas:

The "Hill Houses" are Brooklands, Fircroft, and Highfield; The "Town Houses" are School House, Lorne House, West Deyne (1859) and West Bank; the "Country Houses" are Meadhurst and Farleigh.

There are six girls' boarding houses: Johnson's, The Lodge (sixth form only), Fairfield, New House, Constables and Samworths opened in 2001 being built as the first house for girls aged 13 to 18. It was named for the Samworth Brothers, Old Uppinghamians who helped to finance the construction.

Houses are typically smart Victorian buildings and are usually home to between 50 and 60 children (45 in the case of the sixth-form girls' houses). House prefects are chosen by the housemaster of each house.

Sport and music are typically strong, in 2010 a new sports centre was opened by Seb Coe. Uppingham teams do well against their sporting rivals Oakham, Rugby, Bedford and Stowe. The school has excellent music facilities with significant participation throughout the school strongly encouraged.

Famous Alumni are many and from a wide range of areas

Stephen Dorrell (MP); John Schlesinger (Film Director); Rick Stein (Chef); Donald and Malcolm Campbell (World Speed Record Holders); Jonathan Agnew (Cricket); of the new sports centre; Stephen Fry (Actor); Boris Karloff (Actor); Charles Dunstone and David Ross (Carphone Warehouse); Mark Haddon (Author); James Averdieck (founder of Gü Puds); John Suchet (TV), Johnny Vaughan (comedian) Edward Timpson (MP); Jennifer Willott (MP); Mimi Poskitt (Theatre Director); Dan Hipkiss (Rugby Player); Harry Judd (Musician & member of McFly), Alex Davies and Ed Minton (Musicians and members of up and coming band Elliot Minor).

WELLINGTON COLLEGE

Crowthorne

Berkshire RG45 7PU

www.wellington-college.berks.sch.uk

01344 444000

THIS famous educational establishment which has a long and distinguished military tradition was founded during the Victorian expansion of the public school system in 1859 in honour of the Duke of Wellington. Situated conveniently on the outskirts of Crowthorne a village in Berkshire, approximately 9 miles south of Junction 10 on the M4, the school is easily accessible from London and the Home Counties. The magnificent redbrick buildings surrounded by a sea of green and immaculately kept grounds provide a most idyllic setting for the pupils which now number almost a thousand.

Not so very long ago Wellington College was a major public school struggling to keep up with the best. Numbers were dwindling, morale was low and parents were looking elsewhere for their children's education. Then in 2005 Anthony Seldon their present Headmaster took over at the helm and the school has undergone a major revolution. The high profile and media savvy Dr Seldon who had spruced things up at Brighton College before coming to Wellington hit the ground running and he is still burning rubber. Hardly a week seems to go by without some mention in the press of Wellington College launching an exciting venture or introducing new ideas into education. He is of course also a famous political author having written books on Tony Blair and John Major and his frequent appearances on television have made him a household name.

Like all good leaders he posses excellent communication and people skills as well as the ability to delegate appropriately. Rumours abound that a career in politics awaits this talented man. However, many believe that he is unlikely to abandon ship until Wellington is firmly re-established as a premier league public school.

Under the brilliant guidance of Dr Seldon Wellington has been transformed from an "also ran" to one of the most popular public schools in Britain. Pupil numbers have shot up from 690 in 2005 to 997 in 2011 and I am reliably told that they are planning to admit 1112 pupils in 2012. This is truly a spectacular reversal of fortune and Seldon and his team deserve full credit for what they have achieved. Admission to Wellington has become much more competitive of late and there are now four applicants (and growing) per place. All candidates are assessed aged 11, two years before entry. The pre-entry assessment consists of an interview, prep school reference and a formal aptitude test. See website for further details about the entry assessment or speak to the Registrar. Pupils who are unsuccessful may be placed on a waiting list or politely told to look elsewhere. Moreover, the Common Entrance bar has been raised and now most pupils are expected to obtain an average pass of 65% compared with only 55% five years ago. However, candidates who score 60% at Common Entrance but have something else to offer the school in sport, music or drama will not be turned away. Wellington is now fully co-educational and the aim is to admit 60% boys and 40% girls thus retaining its identity as a predominantly boys school. Naturally, this will help Wellington maintain its reputation as a top rugby playing school.

Schools don't become popular simply because they have charismatic headmasters. Great facilities, sporting reputations, traditional values etc are all important but, the major yardstick now used by many to assess the quality of a private school is its academic achievements and entry into Russell Group universities. Seldon clearly understood this and in a very short period seems to have put in place the radical changes needed to haul Wellington out of the morass of academic mediocrity towards the top of the heap. Last year the school achieved its best ever A-Level results with an A/B grade pass rate of 93%. This may not be on par with Westminster, Winchester or Eton but it is as good as what was achieved at Harrow, Radley, Rugby, Marlborough, Charterhouse and Tonbridge. On a less cheerful note the Oxbridge "hit rate" at around 10% could do with some improvement when compared with 18% for Radley, 18% for Harrow, 34% for Eton and Winchester, and an astonishing 48% for Westminster. In addition the introduction of the A* grade at A-Level will allow parents to assess the academic prowess of a particular school more closely than had previously been the case. In this respect Wellington hopes to improve on last year's satisfactory but not spectacular A* pass rate. Furthermore, the Financial Times 2011 A level league tables which concentrates mainly on the harder subjects such as maths, English, history and sciences at the expense of softer subjects such as media studies, placed Wellington considerably lower than some of its rivals at 220th. Recently the school has added the I.B to its curriculum and it is hoped that this will steadily grow in popularity. Interestingly the head of Sixth Form told us that medical schools find the breadth of the I.B more attractive than A-Levels and in future this qualification may prove to be more suitable for entry into medicine.

Up until a few years ago Wellington was a conventional boys only boarding school. Things have changed somewhat, and nowadays it is more of a mixed bag. There are girls of course, at all levels and up to 20% of the intake is made up of day pupils who have their own House where they can do prep, rest or socialise before returning home. Furthermore, in keeping with modern trends, the school virtually empties on Saturday afternoons as the majority of boarders head back to their families for a roast lunch and hopefully a trip down to Chelsea to mingle with like minded public school kids. Thoroughly refreshed or totally partied out, the boarding crew return on Sunday evening for Chapel Service. The fact that pupils can spend 24 hours with family and friends away from the school also appeals to parents and teachers. As one master put it "keeping teenagers cooped up in school on Saturday evenings can be a recipe for trouble".

Probably because Wellington is not a full boarding school many of its pupils come from London (especially SW) and the Home Counties. It has of course its own feeder prep, Eagle House, which still sends large numbers to the College. However, these days attending Eagle House does not automatically guarantee a place at Wellington. Interestingly, but perhaps not surprisingly, well known boys only boarding preps such as Ludgrove, Summer Fields and Sunningdale seem to send only a handful of boys to Wellington. Eton and Radley seem to be the most common destinations. Based on these figures, one can only assume that parents who seek an education along the lines of the traditional single sex full boarding model are not attracted to Wellington's more contemporary and progressive approach. On the other hand, the reputedly more "modern" London day preps have been won over by Seldon and are sending an increasing number of pupils to Wellington.

Mention Wellington to any group of upper middle class fifty something and somewhere along the line strong military tradition etc.

comes into the conversation. This is hardly surprising since this school is well known for having churned out famous army officers who have shown immense courage on the battle fields of Europe and beyond. However, although modern day Wellington may still take the CCF seriously the military influence is now far less pronounced than it used to be. That said, one must not forget that to date, 14 old boys have been awarded the Victoria Cross. Bearing in mind that this school is only 152 years old, this is quite an achievement. True, Eton, Harrow and Haileybury have had greater success with 36, 19 and 17 V.Cs. respectively but, Eton of course is a larger school. Commendably, Wellington still continues to offer support to our Armed Forces and subject to entry requirement being met, financial awards exist at this school which provide very generous remission for sons and daughters of deceased military servicemen and others who have died in acts of selfless bravery.

Wellington's reputation as a strong sporting school is richly deserved. Rugby remains a great passion and it is played to a very high level. This school has always been "the one to beat" on the rugby field and over the years has had great success in The Daily Mail Cup. However, now that girls make up a sizeable chunk of the schools intake their rugby team is probably less formidable. That said, results are still highly impressive and needle matches against other top rugby playing schools provide great opportunities for the testosterone charged boys to channel their energy into something constructive. While on the subject of competitive rugby matches, in 2008 a player emerged from the scrum in a Wellington-Marlborough game sporting teeth marks in the vicinity of one of his ears! This incidence was widely reported in the press and not surprisingly led to a war of words between the two schools.

As one would expect from a major public school charging fees of almost £30,000 per annum Wellington caters brilliantly for most activities including music, art and drama. It's lavishly illustrated prospectus states that whether the interest is in classical, rock, jazz or pop, Wellington provides an enormously diverse music programme. The orchestra is conducted by the celebrated Hilary Davan Wetton and performances are held throughout the year encompassing venues such as St Pauls Cathedral and St John Smith Square. The quality of art work is also highly impressive and can be seen throughout the College during any visit. Wellington has an established Artist-in-Residence scheme where distinguished practitioners work alongside pupils.

On a glorious spring day in May 2011, with the Berkshire countryside looking at its best my wife and I visited Wellington College to find out what makes this place tick. Having got lost within the village of Crowthorne, after some help from the locals, we finally found ourselves at the entrance of the College motoring along the impressive drive towards the imposing redbrick buildings. A game of cricket against Bradfield was in full swing but it was too early to forecast the likely outcome. Neatly dressed fresh faced youngsters were milling around being very helpful and talking positively about their school. Everyone seemed happy and at ease with themselves and the whole place had a sense of serene gentility. Rather surprisingly, when we visited the dining room we were astonished to discover that the girls sat at one end of the dining hall and boys at the other! We were assured that this is not school policy and boys and girls are free to share dining tables if they so wish. We were also shown class rooms used by sixth formers where large oval tables dominated the rooms. Apparently, the purpose of these tables is to allow pupils and teachers to sit together in one large group so as to create a more relaxed teaching environment. This idea has come across from America where it is has been a feature at famous private schools for some time.

In summary an excellent and forward looking co-educational establishment which is now greatly in demand. We were highly impressed with what is on offer and would thoroughly recommend this place to anyone who is looking for a public school education with a more progressive and liberal slant.

WESTMINSTER SCHOOL

Westminster

London SW1P 3PF

www.westminster.org.uk

0207 963 1000

LOCATED in central London adjacent to Westminster Abbey and within a short walk from the Houses of Parliament, this ancient educational establishment can trace its origins back to 1179, when the Benedictine monks of Westminster Abbey were required by Pope Alexander III to provide a small charity school. After the dissolution of the monastery by Henry the VIII in 1540, the schools survival was personally ensured by the King. His daughter Queen Elizabeth I drew up statutes in 1560 and the constitution included a requirement that the school should educate forty scholars. 1560 is taken to be the year of foundation and Elizabeth I as the school's foundress.

Westminster enjoys a richly deserved reputation as the most academic school in Britain. Astonishingly, but perhaps unsurprisingly, the school has topped the highly respected Financial Times Academic League Tables for the last five years. The school offers both A-Level and Pre-U but not the IB. Virtually all the alumni head for higher education and the Oxbridge success rate remains enviably high with just under 50% of the pupils gaining entry into our two most famous universities. Those who choose or are forced to look elsewhere tend to turn their attention to other top ranked universities which include Imperial College, LSE and UCL. Prestigious American universities such as Harvard, Yale and Princeton are also popular destinations. Generally speaking provincial

241

British universities tend not to be automatic first choices, but Westminster scholars do pop up at places such as Bristol, Durham or Warwick where they tend to seek out popular subjects such as law, medicine or economics. Such stellar achievements however, can only be obtained if the raw material is of the very best quality and the standard of teaching top drawer.

Entry into Westminster is highly selective and based entirely on academic ability. This is uncompromising and apparently no concessions are made for boys who may be first rate sportsmen but fail to demonstrate the necessary intellectual qualities deemed essential for survival at this school. The general view is that pupils would probably not be happy or thrive at Westminster if they were not passionate about studying, learning and competing to the highest level. Achieving high grades in examinations and winning places at top universities seems to be the overriding priority for the vast majority. This of course does not mean that extra- curricular activities are not important. The school may not play rugby, but a variety of other sports are played to a competitive level even if some parents feel that they could be taken a little more seriously. Moreover, the music department is one of the best in the country and drama is also highly respected. Interestingly, unlike many other top public schools who offer sports, drama or technology scholarships this is not the case at Westminster. At this school only academic and music scholarship are on offer. Furthermore, the school is increasingly adopting a "needs blind" policy which means that financial assistance will be offered to any pupil deemed worthy of a place even if the parents lack the financial means to pay the school fees. To its credit Westminster makes great effort to raise money for these bursaries and some of the fund raising events have generated very impressive sums of money.

Boys are admitted to Westminster at 13 via Common Entrance, with the pass mark set at a minimum of 70%, or Scholarship Examination. Pre testing and interviews are carried out at the 11+ stage when the boys are in Year 6. Over 400 pupils will be tested for the 120 available places. Prospective candidates will be tested in Mathematics, English and Verbal Reasoning. An interview and prep school report also form part of the assessment. Boys who have won academic scholarships (Queen Scholars) are entitled to a very generous 50% remission in fees but are all required to board although they are allowed to go home on Saturday afternoons and spend the weekend with their families if they so wish. As is the case at Winchester and Eton the scholars at Westminster, which number 40 in total, all live together in the same house, generally referred to as "College". At this stage it is worth stressing that although Westminster is predominantly a day school, 185 pupils out of a total of 740 are boarders. Girls enter the school in the Sixth Form only and the 70 or so girls can be either boarders or day pupils. Moreover, although the girls have added an exciting dimension to this vibrant school there are no immediate plans for Westminster to become fully co-educational.

How do Westminster boys differ from Etonians? This may seem an unusual question, but interestingly enough I have met many parents who have sought such an answer. Unlike Eton which is a full boarding single sex school, Westminster is largely a day school with a co-educational sixth form. Day pupils come from all over London and the majority use public transport arriving via St James's Park or Westminster underground stations. Not infrequently, on route to school, these metropolitan savvy kids walk past groups of people demonstrating outside the House of Commons. Westminster is very much a liberal cosmopolitan school reflecting the face of modern London. Eton on the other hand, could well be on another planet. Apart from both schools being extremely expensive (boarding fees £30000) and achieving spectacularly high academic results, there are few other similarities. The full boarding nature of Eton means that Etonians are largely confined to a closeted life within the schools perimeter. Sportsmen are revered at Eton and rugby, rowing and cricket are taken extremely seriously. Etonians may come from London but many originate from the Home Counties and the Shires. The landed gentry and the aristocracy still have a visible presence at Eton where tails, top hats, pinstriped trousers etc. form part of their daily uniform. Furthermore, activities associated with upper class families such as polo, shooting and fly fishing are well catered for at Eton and reasonably popular. In general, my understanding is that Westminster pupils are a diverse bunch and not terribly easy to pigeon-hole. Etonians on the other hand, are more definable and rightly or wrongly still tarred with the brush of snobbery.

Westminster is clearly an academic school which achieves the best results in the land. However extra-curricular activities such as music, drama, sport, expeditions and debating are just as important. Two afternoons a week are set aside for games and the school has its own playing fields at Vincent Square which I have been told is the largest open space in Central London apart from the Royal Parks. Historically, the principle sports at Westminster are rowing (known as water), football and cricket, and the school can justifiably claim an important place in history in all three of these sports. There is a boat house in Putney and the origin of the competitive rowing go back to the races between Westminster and Eton in the early 19th Century. Also the first known cricket match between public schools was Westminster v. Harrow in 1796. In 1863 Westminster competed against Charterhouse in the first ever school football match and the two schools are credited for devising the off-side rule which was then adopted by the Football Association. There is no rugby at Westminster and this can work both ways. There are boys who rejoice at the idea of no muddy scrums or nasty tackles and others, who having considered Westminster, opted for Eton where rugby is well established.

Music is taken extremely seriously and holds a central place in the life of Westminster School. The majority of pupils play at least one instrument but many two or more. Up to six music scholarships to the value of 25% of the day or boarding fee are awarded annually to boys entering the school at 13. The school has a long standing musical tradition which encompasses names such as Henry Purcell, Andrew Lloyd Webber, Adrian Boult, Roger Norrington, Ian Bostridge, Dido and Mika. Music is offered as a subject at GCSE and A-Level and there are numerous concerts of which some take place at Westminster Abbey. Drama and art are given high priorities at Westminster and the quality of their theatrical production has been described as excellent. One would expect no less from a school whose old pupils include Imogen Stubbs, Helena Bonham Carter, Peter Brook, Peter Ustinov and Sir John Gielgud. Famous playwrights of the past include Ben Jonson and John Dryden

Historically, Westminster has had a close affinity to Church and State. This has naturally been helped by the schools proximity to Westminster Abbey and the Houses of Parliament. Westminster pupils I believe still set their wrist watches by glancing at Big Ben! Apparently, politics is a serious subject at this school and many of the children seem to enjoy the cut and thrust of animated political debates. Within the present coalition government of 2011 Westminster old boys include Nick Clegg the Deputy Prime Minister and Chris Huhne the Cabinet Minister at the Department of Energy who recently resigned. The legendary Anthony Wedgwood Benn (commonly known as Tony Benn) is also a product of this great school. He of course, famously gave up his aristocratic title to become a Labour MP and subsequently a leading figure on the left wing of his party. The ebullient and highly intellectual political heavyweight Nigel Lawson, who was Chancellor of the Exchequer in Margaret Thatcher's cabinet, was also educated at Westminster. Eton and Harrow may have produced more Prime Ministers but this school has had more than its fair share of famous politicians and will undoubtedly continue to play an influential role in the House of Commons well into the future.

On a grey, early December day in 2011, my wife and I visited this famous school having travelled via the Metropolitan and Jubilee lines from our home on the Herts/Bucks border. Like the pupils who attend this school we also walked past demonstrators in Parliament Square on our short journey from Westminster underground station to Vincent Square. During our visit the present headmaster, Dr Stephen Spurr, very kindly gave up two hours of his precious time during which he eloquently outlined the many exciting features associated with this school. We greatly enjoyed chatting to the charismatic Dr Spurr and found him most helpful.

Having not considered Westminster as a potential school for our two boys, the main objective of the visit was to research material for this book. We live in the Chilterns some 30 miles from Central London and our lives revolve around rural pursuits. Boarding schools like Radley, Eton or Stowe are more suitable options for us. However, by the time we had departed from Vincent Square our perceptions of Westminster had altered substantially. This place has so much more to offer other than just brilliant academic results and we now fully realize how fortunate our metropolitan friends are in having such a fantastic school on their doorsteps.

WINCHESTER COLLEGE

Winchester

Hampshire SO23 9NA

www.winchestercollege.co.uk

01962 621100

THIS ancient and famous boarding school was founded in 1382 by the Bishop of Winchester, William of Wykeham. Nestled within the pretty Hampshire town of Winchester along the banks of a celebrated trout stream, Winchester College remains the oldest school in England still operating from its original site. The splendid medieval buildings known as College are reserved for the 70 Kings Scholars or "Collegemen" as they are known at Winchester, who have all been selected by competitive examination. The remaining 610 boys who are generally referred to as "Commoners," live in 10 boarding houses, all within easy walking distance of the college and its facilities. Winchester, together with Eton, Harrow and Westminster, constitute a quartet of elite public schools whose reputations stretch well beyond our domestic boundaries.

With only 680 boys, virtually all boarders, Winchester feels less imposing and more intimate than a large school like Eton. Furthermore, unlike Eton or Harrow where boys wear traditional school uniforms, Wykemists can wear more or less what they fancy so long as it involves jacket and tie. When I visited the school I was most impressed with the smartly dressed boys, clad in tweed jackets, blazers or suits all finished off with ties to express their individuality. However a touch of sartorial tradition is maintained with the 70 scholars who are required to wear a black gown. Winchester College is a niche school which appeals to academic high flyers that don't mind conversing in Latin amongst themselves or bury the heads in books on route to Oxbridge. As the old saying goes: you can always tell a Wykemist but, you can't tell him much!

The main criterion for admission remains academic prowess with social background being largely irrelevant. The Headmaster was keen to point out that the school is remarkably unpretentious and unlikely to attract social climbers. Unlike Harrow for example, whose alumni have included the present Duke of Westminster and Duke of Bedford, Winchester has never been hugely popular with the aristocracy. Future Dukes, Earls and Viscounts are conspicuous by their absence. Another important point to consider is that rugby, a game that often goes hand in hand with private education, is not played at Winchester and this may be a significant factor in choosing or not choosing Winchester. Cricket, on the other hand, is played to a high standard and up until 1855 Winchester was one of the Lord's Schools, competing in the triangular cricket tournament with Eton and Harrow. Why Winchester dropped out of this tournament is not clear, but traditions die hard at this school and the cricket First XI is still known as "Lord's".

Winchester College is one of the most academic public schools in Britain and remains an attractive proposition for intelligent boys who wish to board. Unsurprisingly A-Level results are phenomenally good and in 2011 the school was ranked 7th in the Financial Times performance tables for independent schools. Of its rivals only Westminster which was 1st and St Paul's, 3rd were ranked higher. This of course is hardly surprising. These highly selective cosmopolitan institutions are predominantly day schools and Westminster also has the added advantage of a co-educational sixth form. Winchester on the other hand, as a full boarding single sex school in the heart of Hampshire has fewer applicants to choose from but, still manages to deliver stellar results. Furthermore, Winchester's ability to send large numbers to some of the best universities in Britain and North America is also highly commendable. Last year 37% of Wykemists went to Oxbridge/UCL and the rest to other famous institutions such as Imperial College, Bristol, London School of Economics and Edinburgh. The historical association with Oxford remains particularly strong which is not surprising since Winchester College was founded in conjunction with New College Oxford. American Ivy League Colleges such as Harvard, Yale and Princeton are becoming increasingly popular as they regarded by many as a good alternative to Oxbridge.

The present economic environment may have affected numbers at some schools but this is most definitely not the case at Winchester which is now running slightly above full capacity with 690 boys. As one would expect competition for entry is fierce and there are now four candidates per place. Last year boys were admitted from 126 prep schools from all over the world, with 12% of the pupils originating from countries outside the European Union. The vast majority of contemporary Wykehamists come from homes within the South of England, with Scotland, Yorkshire and East Anglia featuring considerably less than they once did. This is understandable since nowadays parents prefer to be closer to their children for a variety of reasons.

The admission of boys to Winchester is largely in the hands of Housemasters who will interview and test all the boys registered for their particular house. A boy can be registered as a prospective member of a Commoner boarding house from the age of eight and when he reaches 11, he and his parents will be invited to meet the Housemaster. Conditional offers are made on the basis of the Housemasters interview, which includes school reports and a written test. These offers are on condition that the boy subsequently passes Winchesters own Entrance Examination, which, according to the Headmaster, is similar to Common Entrance but more "grown up". Last year only two boys who sat this examination failed to reach the required standards and were not admitted to the school. The Winchester Entrance Examination takes place in May of the year of entry. This procedure does not apply to Scholars who are selected by competitive examination. Candidates who are successful in winning a scholarship are entitled to a reduction in their fees of 25%. In case of financial need, the school may remit all or part of the remaining fees.

This school may have a superb reputation for academic excellence but its overall objective is to offer a well rounded education to its pupils. With this in mind boys at Winchester meet up for Division (Div) periods on a daily basis with their Div Dons. These lessons are usually 40 minutes long but on some days can go on to 80 minutes. This is an unexamined program of study covering an extremely wide range of subjects, designed to enrich the learning experience without the added pressure of end point assessment. Div as one can imagine, can lead almost anywhere, and what is discussed depends largely on the interests of the Div Dons and the boys. Div is an important part of a boys education at Winchester and it is taken very seriously, whether the subject for discussion happens to be the Gulf War, plays by Tom Stoppard, the music of Bach or the history of cricket.

The music department at Winchester enjoys a tremendous reputation amongst public schools and some believe it is probably one of the best in the country. Music has been central to this school ever since its foundation in 1382 when William of Wykeham made provision for 16 choir boys. The vast majority of boys play at least one instrument and many play two or three. The school currently has over 60 music scholars and some of the boys are known to arrive at Winchester from their prep schools having obtained Grade 8 in piano! When it comes to sport, however, some parents tend to view Winchester as a school where games are not taken very seriously. Whether this is true or not is debatable. It is worth noting that in the first year PE is compulsory as is Wednesday afternoon sport. Thereafter three sessions of "effort" as it is known to the boys must be completed weekly and signed off by a sports master. These activities are entirely up to each individual boy's choice. As mentioned earlier rugby is not played at this school but all the boys are encouraged to play Winchester Football in the spring term. This game is not played at any other schools and therefore most matches are between the houses which are naturally fiercely competitive. Winchester Football is considered to be a cross between football and rugby, and it is played with a soccer ball but includes rugby-like scrums, in fact similar to the Eton field game. Ordinary football, the type played by the likes of Chelsea and Manchester United, is also popular at Winchester and so far this year they've had 13 wins, 7 losses and 2 draws. Furthermore, I have been reliably informed by the school that Winchester excels in minor sports such as Racquets and Basketball which should not be discounted. Whilst on the subject of minor sport it is worth noting that there is no polo at Winchester. However, fly-fishing for trout on the River Itchen as well as clay-pigeon shooting are keenly taught and greatly enjoyed by the alumni who have an interest in field sports.

I would like to finish this article by quoting from the Winchester College website outlining life beyond Winchester:

"When they reach university, whether with gap year experience or not, Wykehamists are well equipped to work reliably, learn independently and contribute both socially and intellectually during the next stage of their continuing education. They have, after all, been imbued with a love of learning which will stay with them for the rest of their lives. You will find Wykehamists in almost every walk of professional, creative and entrepreneurial life, and what marks them out is not any clichéd "public school" veneer of confidence, but an understated, self-assured competence and ability to work with many different groups of people in many different situations. Those are the qualities implied in the motto *Manners Makyth Man.* They thrive on bringing their disciplined minds to bear on a problem and to finding its solution."

In summary a world famous school catering for some of our brightest boys destined for great and exciting careers.

WYCOMBE ABBEY

High Wycombe

Buckinghamshire HP11 1PE

www.wycombeabbey.com

01494 520381

Heather Morley

IF you are reading this guide you are probably in one of three camps. Either you are in the education business and are checking out the competition (or in some cases, what we say about your place of work!) or you are a parent or you are a pupil. My own perspective is that of a parent with two daughters who are approaching the age when they will switch to senior school. So this is the question I am trying to answer: Would I want my daughter to attend Wycombe Abbey?

The thing about "Wycombe" – insiders don't extend the name by adding "Abbey" very often – is that its reputation precedes it. Talk to people and they will say that it is an academic hothouse; some girls are under such pressure that they become ill or choose to rebel; that only incredibly gifted girls should attempt to gain access. Certainly if you look at its academic credentials it looks intimidating – 99% GCSE grades are A/A*, over 90% gain A/A* at A-level and 40% achieve Oxbridge places. But what is it like on the inside? Why is it that all the girls I see around the place are so happy and normal-looking? Why was it given the accolade of Sunday Times Independent School of The Year in 2010, for the second time in a decade?

Wycombe Abbey was founded in 1896 by pioneer educationalist Dame Frances Dove to give girls "the opportunity of a Christian liberal education". Sitting in a stunning park of some 167 sloping acres in central High Wycombe, it is fronted by an imposing grey castellated mansion built by James Wyatt in 1798 for the first Lord Carrington.

Currently there are 560 girls in the school, of which about 18% are foreign nationals. Girls come from all over Britain (largeish number from London, according to one pupil) and otherwise from France, Italy, Switzerland, Monaco, Russia, India, China, USA, Canada, Nigeria, Iran and Thailand. Headmistress Cynthia Hall (more of her later) vastly enjoys seeing girls of all nationalities fully-integrated and wandering around the school with their arms around each other, almost like a mini UN, only more friendly!

Its facilities are first class, comparing very favourably with other schools of this ilk. The Sports Centre, built in 2004 boasts a 25m indoor swimming pool, sports hall, dance studio, climbing wall, squash courts, etc. Countless tennis courts and lacrosse pitches pepper the landscape alongside mature trees, a lake and evidence of a diligent team of gardeners.

Advocates of the school wax lyrical about not only the sports facilities and dedicated staff, but also of the results achieved by the girls. One current pupil says, when asked why she chose Wycombe above comparable schools - "we're just better ... a strong history of beating them in sporting events such as lacrosse, netball and tennis". Looking for evidence of a more objective nature, I asked for a list of girls who currently represent their country at sport (not a question you would think to ask at most schools. It is symptomatic of Wycombe that it seems natural to ask it here). Lacrosse is a big deal – eight girls play for England

Under 17's and three for Under 19's, plus many younger ones are involved with Regional Centex (the training ground for national players). One girl is on the edges of national Netball. Another hopes to represent Spain in swimming at the next Olympics. Two others are national-level riders. A nationally-ranked table tennis player. County-level sportswomen are too numerous to mention. Wow. With 30 different sports to choose from, they claim that there is something for everyone. I believe them.

The chapel is a particular feature of the school, designed by the Arts and Crafts architect W.D. Caroe (who also created the boarding houses that abut the main road leading up and out of High Wycombe). It offers an architecturally-pleasing place of worship, sanctuary and quiet reflection as well as a meeting place for the whole school.

There are nine senior boarding houses – Airlie, Barry, Butler, Campbell, Cloister, Pitt, Rubens, Shelburne and Wendover – that accommodate girls in Years 8-12. 11 year-old newcomers are housed in cosy Junior House whilst Upper Sixth formers are esconced in Clarence for the duration of their A-level tribulations. Allocation of senior house happens *before* a girl arrives at the school for the first time and family members *may* share the same house, even after an interval of a considerable number of years. The school makes a big deal of the importance of community – the girls spend two thirds of their year at Wycombe so it seems reasonable to do so. Unusually, the convention is that girls mix freely between year groups. This is a refreshing change from when I was at school and one looked up or down at other kids simply because of age. In real life we mix with lots of people of any age and to start this at school seems eminently sensible.

Ask the girls what they enjoy most about life at Wycombe Abbey and they will very often talk about the Music, Dance and Drama on offer.

There is a superb Performing Arts Centre where the girls can engage in Ballet, Street Dance, Modern and Tap. A vast array of musical instruments can be learnt. The annual school Gazette lists some impressive exam grades – 16 grade 8 exams were taken in 2009/10 and nine of those achieved a Distinction. Boarding houses compete with each other in the annual Drama competition, Music competition and countless other plays and recitals occur during the action-packed year. A highlight has been the "Wycombe's Got Talent" competition. However one pupil commented that despite her enjoyment of the "endless choice" of extra-curricular activities, making the most of these can lead to a certain level of exhaustion.

What kind of girls go to Wycombe Abbey? One pupil noted that most are from the "upper end of the social spectrum" although she rightly pointed out that this would apply at most public schools. Whilst she finds a few to be a tad snooty, she says that "most are genuine, down-to-earth and not as money-oriented as one might think. This was one of my worries when I was applying to the school but I have been proven wrong!" A new parent commented that Wycombe is "a place where I can speak my mind, I'm not worried about saying 'the right thing'". I doubt the girls are stuck for words at their socials with Eton, Harrow, Radley, Winchester, Abingdon, Papplewick, Ludgrove and indeed the excellent local boys' grammar, Royal Grammar School (with whom they share a Management Conference, celebratory ball and university preparation sessions).

The girls who thrive here are clearly a forthright and straight lot. Pupils of my acquaintance at the school seem to be able to stand on their own two feet somewhat earlier than others; they are not princesses who are excessively concerned about their appearance; they are independent-minded; they talk to me as an equal, not as if I am some irrelevant ancient;

they read a lot, and widely; they have a broad range of extra-curricular interests; they are very often quirky (one recently successful applicant writes screenplays at the age of *12*!); without boasting they are often precociously talented (my friend's daughter is bilingual, plays competitive netball and happens to have Grade 3 guitar and saxophone – all at the age of 11); their energy comes from within, rather than from pushy parents; they are steady. I asked a parent what sort of girl would succeed at Wycombe – "I do feel that there is a type of girl who thrives at the school, academically capable, socially comfortable and with specific interests that may be broad or deep". So who does not do well at the school? "Someone who isn't prepared to work and who is not willing to involve themselves in school life" says one pupil. Or as a parent puts it: "Someone who gets lost in a crowd or who approaches academic life as an obstacle rather than a challenge". Well that sorts that out, then!

There is one key element that I have not yet mentioned – the staff. The perception is of a stuffy, blue-stockinged institution designed to cloister away girls until they are set free at 18. This is totally blown away by the refreshing and caring individuals that I have met at the school. Headmistress Cynthia Hall studied Literature at Oxford, edited "Isis" in her second year and then followed her father into teaching. She started at a school in Peterborough in 1974 and has taught at all-girls independent schools (including St Paul's) ever since. Her previous incarnation was a 15-year stint as Headmistress at St Helen's and St Katherine's in Abingdon (known affectionately as "St HellKats"!). A self-confessed liberal, she says the worst part of her job is the disciplining of wayward pupils – "sometimes necessary". Her favourite part is leading 11 year-olds through the garden of her beloved literature, fascinated by the interests and observations of her bright young charges. This is not a Head who is naturally scary. Mrs Hall is a charming woman who is obviously thoughtful, enthusiastic and in it to do some good. She derives much pleasure from listing the achievements of her girls, and is very aware of the process that takes them from innocent, wide-eyed 11 year-olds to confident, supremely well-educated young ladies. On the subject of eminent ex-pupils, the list she gave me featured few familiar names – Dame Elizabeth Butler-Sloss, Frances Osborne and Penelope Fizgerald were the ones I recognised. What I loved was the fact that pupils revere their antecedents for their intrepid natures and disrespect for the rules that limit women in their ambition. The list includes actresses, playwrights, journalists, artists, designers, sportswomen, authors and politicians – brave innovators every one.

Other staff come in for a similar level of approval. There is undoubtedly kudos in the teaching world accorded to those who practise their profession here. Academic results prove their ability, but the smiles, admiration and indeed fondness that girls have for their teaching and house staff speak volumes. One new parent even praises the attitude of the Custodians (security men) at the gate – "I think the security staff are extremely friendly. Might not sound important, but to receive a smile when arriving at the gate after a long drive dropping your girl back makes all the difference!"

So would I want my daughter to attend Wycombe Abbey? There is absolutely no doubt that this is the perfect school, if you are the right sort of girl. It is also apparent that the admissions process selects the right sort of girls very effectively. There are, of course, some individuals who somehow slip through the net and don't have a great time here. It is a school that keeps girls younger for longer (impromptu picnics in the grounds, serious emphasis on tobogganing when it snows, high levels of adherence to make-up, uniform and jewellery rules, strict controls on venturing out into High Wycombe). A handful - about ten a year - leave for co-ed schools in the sixth form. Mostly to Westminster, Magdalen College School, more rarely Marlborough or Rugby. Perhaps they find it a bit constraining to be under such careful supervision.

I came away from Wycombe Abbey with a serious case of envy for the girls who pass through its doors. Its slightly austere appearance belies a warm and friendly place where girls are taught that the world is out there to be discovered. It does not tell them that they are better than anyone else, but that they must do something useful with their lives – and to have bucket-loads of fun on the way. Gosh I'd love to send my daughters there, I'd better start saving!